Voices from the Garden

Voices from the Garden

Stories of Becoming a Vegetarian

Edited by Daniel and Sharon Towns

Lantern Books • New York
A Division of Booklight Inc.

2001
Lantern Books
One Union Square West, Suite 201
New York, NY 10003

Printed in the United States of America

Library of Congress Cataloging-in-Publication Data

Voices from the garden : stories of becoming a vegetarian / edited by Daniel and Sharon Towns.
    p. cm.
Includes bibliographical references (p.).
ISBN 1-930051-80-8 (pbk.)
    1. Vegetarianism. I. Towns, Daniel. II. Towns, Sharon.

TX392.7.V65 2001
641.5'636—dc21

200138433

Table of Contents

❧ *Foreword* ❧

HOWARD LYMAN

Reading *Voices From the Garden* brought back many memories of the time I made the biggest change of my life. Eleven years ago, I decided to quit eating meat. The change was a lot more traumatic for me because I was a fourth generation cattle rancher.

I was raised in Montana, definitely meat-and-potatoes country. The only vegetarian I had met was named Atlantis, and you can bet that both her name and diet seemed a little over the edge to me. The only reason I considered becoming a vegetarian was because my blood pressure was sky high, my weight was well over three hundred pounds, and my cholesterol was over three hundred. I would eat lunch and my nose would bleed. I was a heart attack waiting to happen.

I decided to quit eating meat, but decided not to tell anyone, so if I failed no one would know. When we spend the majority of our lives being told that eating meat will make us big, strong, and healthy, and all of our family and friends are happily eating meat, planning to become vegetarian is a daunting lifestyle change.

I became the world's worst vegetarian, subsisting for a year on a diet of little more than lettuce and dairy products. I lost some weight, my blood pressure dropped some, and my cholesterol decreased a little. I thought that if I could improve my health a little by being the world's worst vegetarian, how much more could I accomplish if I did it right.

On a vegan diet I lost over one hundred twenty pounds, my blood pressure went to normal, and my cholesterol dropped to one hundred thirty five. I felt so good that I wanted to change every one of my friends and family into card-carrying vegans. To my surprise, they didn't want to hear what I had to say. It was my first real lesson in the power of the fork. *Voices from the Garden* showed me the ways other people dealt with the same problem I had faced. Many of them handled it much better than I did.

Reading this book will arm you with the knowledge to change the world without destroying yourself in the process. This book is good for the environment, good for animals, and good for your health. Read it and live.

❧ *Preface* ❧
INGRID NEWKIRK

How do we become who we are? As this book shows, everyone evolves differently and their stories are all interesting.

A nurse and friend of mine at People for the Ethical Treatment of Animals (PETA) looked down at her beloved cat "Beanie" one day and "for no apparent reason," suddenly thought, "If I wouldn't dream of eating Beanie, why on Earth do I eat other animals?" Another friend was stopped short when a hunter she was berating for his blood "sport" asked her, "Do you eat chicken? Well, what's the difference between paying someone to kill a chicken and me shooting the quail? Isn't a deer the same as a cow?" My friend was tongue-tied. After all, what could she say, as the realization dawned on her that he was right? The suffering endured by animals crammed into pens and cages on factory farms and then suffering the miserable journey in trucks to slaughter make the chickens' and the cows' experience vivid and painful.

A doctor friend on the East Coast had another out-of-the-blue epiphany. He was driving along in his car when he heard a news reporter on the radio describe how people were upset that Vietnamese immigrants might eat dogs. Suddenly, it struck him that it was only a cultural difference that kept most Westerners from including dogs in the long list of animals we eat. He went home and talked to his wife, and they both became vegetarians.

Other people are lucky enough to make the connection earlier in life. Some were children when they realized that the meat on their plates came from the adorable "duckies" and lambs in their storybooks and on their bedroom curtains. Usually, but not always, a parent intervened and forced or persuaded the questioning child to be quiet and eat their dinner. Those children often grow up to think about the issue later in life and, this time, to make their veggie pledge stick.

For me, as you'll read in these pages, it was finding a little abandoned pig on a farm and holding that animal in my arms that helped me put two and two together. I was a very slow learner. I wore fur, fished, and ate almost all the animals you will ever see listed on a menu. All the while, I opened my heart and home to rescued dogs and cats and wildlife and was horrified that, during the war, my grandmother had fed horsemeat to my grandfather, telling him it was beef.

Recently, PETA released an advertisement that shows a chicken staring at a human leg on a plate. The tag line is "Please, try to relate to who's on your plate!"

This book is all about relating. How people began to relate and what it has done to them, emotionally, physically, and spiritually. I hope you enjoy it, pass it on, and write your own story and attach it to the end of the book.

Here's to a good read and truly "good" appetite!

❧ Introduction ❧
DANIEL AND SHARON TOWNS

Our story is probably similar to other vegetarians of like age. Over our twenty-nine-year marriage, we have often experienced the guilt of eating animal flesh and thus attempted vegetarianism. In the 1970s and 1980s, however, our choices were limited and as our meals seemed to become endlessly repetitious, we always resumed eating meat. Our guilt, however, was never assuaged and we knew, ultimately, we would one day give up all forms of animal flesh forever. That day came some eight years ago. We have never regretted our decision and we are proud that we can state with absolute certainty we will never eat meat again.

Credit (and undying gratitude) must be given to Farm Sanctuary in Watkins Glen, New York for helping to make our decision such an easy one. From the co-founders to the interns, the commitment to animal welfare of this organization can never be called into question.

Our activism, though beginning with vegetarianism, has not ended there. Our lives are dedicated to animals: speaking at every opportunity to end the suffering of the companion animals permitted to reproduce over and over again, facing certain extermination in shelters around the world; speaking out for the animals tortured in laboratories every day in the name of "science;" speaking out for the farm animals treated so horribly and slaughtered so inhumanely, just to place dinner on millions of tables; speaking out for the battered and abused circus animals so callously forced to perform as so-called entertainment; and speaking out for the fur animals brutally killed simply for the vanity and shallowness of human beings.

The primary theme of the stories that follow is, of course, vegetarianism. Many of them, however, also touch on other subjects about which those of us in the animal rights movement, feel very strongly. We hope these stories will make you think: the next time you use eye shadow or lipstick, did those products burn the eyes or skin of a laboratory dog or cat? The next time you wash you hair, was that product responsible for the blindness of a laboratory rabbit or monkey? When you put on your fur-trimmed winter jacket, was that mink bashed over the head for your vanity? When you attend a circus, did that elephant being poked, prodded, and hooked make you smile? When you allow your companion animal to have "just one litter" so your children can see the miracle of birth, did you then take your children to the local shelter to witness the horror of death? And, when you take that bite of roast beef, was that cow skinned alive? Think about these things. See animals as they are—living beings who feel pain and have emotions, just as you and I do.

Vegetarianism is on the rise. New vegetarian cookbooks are published every year. On the market now are substitutes for almost every meat product, the majority of which can easily fool even the serious carnivore. Vegetarians are no longer limited to shopping only at their health food store, either. Even your local supermarket is offering more and more vegetarian items.

Try vegetarianism. You will know that you are not contributing to the torture and murder of billions of animals per year. You'll feel better and your conscience will be clear.

Read these stories. But most importantly, *think* about these stories.

Sixty Years of Vegetarianism
MARION FRIEDMAN

A vegetarian for ethical reasons since age eleven (I am now seventy-five), I became vegan about twelve years ago when I attended a national vegetarian seminar that was held in Philadelphia where I learned that there was also cruelty in the attainment of dairy, eggs, honey, wool, etc. The only dairy I really had to give up was butter pecan ice cream, but I now enjoy Tofutti™ or Rice Dream™, which replaces ice cream. I gave up wearing wool and my dress coat is a beautiful cotton velvet swing coat.

My late husband and I were married for thirty-nine years and, although he loved our cats, he did not see the connection in eating other animals and so never became a vegetarian. What he did was eat what I ate at home and he would order chicken, fish, or beef when we ate out, usually twice a week.

I sometimes eat in vegetarian Indian or Chinese restaurants, but often go with friends to non-vegetarian restaurants. I do not make a production of my being vegetarian, nor do I make others feel uncomfortable about it. I either order from the salad bar or eat side dishes such as beet salad, applesauce, etc. In a Middle Eastern restaurant I order a falafel sandwich, which is very tasty with hot sauce.

I have a gentleman friend now who is not vegetarian, but is understanding of my viewpoints, as are many other non-vegetarian friends and relatives, who are all compassionate but do not know (or do not want to know) how animals reach their plates.

I do not make them feel uncomfortable. I have a few vegetarian/vegan friends.

When I go to someone's home for dinner, I usually bring my own food and often bring something I made to share with others. I am not much of a cook, but can make a few potato dishes. I buy much of my food at a natural food store once a week where I can get fresh salad, produce, fruits, and grains. I prefer mostly cold, raw food but also eat some hot, cooked foods like corn on the cob or mashed potatoes. I also buy some food supplies through mail order catalogs. I am a vegetarian for ethical reasons not health reasons, and I do eat some junk food. By ordering from vegetarian catalogs, I am able to eat chocolates, cookies, etc. without worrying about what is in them.

My activism consists mostly of contributing to some animal rights organizations, writing letters about animal issues and legislation to my elected officials, and by handing out literature. I have also purchased over forty copies of *Diet for a New America* by John Robbins and have given them out to various friends. I have also purchased other animal rights books and vegetarian cookbooks to donate to libraries or give as gifts to friends and relatives.

I worked for the University of Pennsylvania for twenty-nine years and, when I retired in November 1995, the school had a big retirement party for me where they included many vegetarian foods.

Since December 1995, I have been a volunteer teacher's aide two days per week at the local elementary school. I assist a second grade teacher and an art teacher. One day, I gave an issue of *The Animals' Agenda* to the school science teacher who said she had never seen the magazine before. I later asked her if she wanted additional copies and she said she did. I now give her my copies when I finish them. This is one way of giving out literature and hoping that something "rubs off" on others.

❧ *How I Became a Vegetarian* ❧
MARU VIGO

To become a vegetarian in a South American country is a difficult task to accomplish. The nasty, unhealthy, and unethical habit of eating meat was another one of the "cultural gifts" that Spaniards brought from Europe in the 1500s. Apart from the occasional dried llama meat that the Incas consumed, the basic diet of the early Peruvians consisted of corn, sweet potatoes, quinoa, beans, ajies (Peruvian chilies), potatoes, and some other legumes and grains. Fed with this diet, the Incas were able to build one of the most important and mighty empires of the Ancient World.

Early Peruvians shared a special attachment to the land that produced all this food so generously. The Earth Mother or Pacha Mama was the materialization of the Divine. It was a living, cosmic being with a physical and spiritual body. The coming of the greedy Spaniards and the imposition of their dietary habits not only disrupted the Inca economy but also damaged the social stratification of the empire. Imposing agricultural and farming methods that were totally inferior to the ones developed by the Incas, the Spanish forced the population to change their natural vegetarian diet to a meat-based diet.

Later on in history, meat consumption became a high status symbol and the basic staple foods consumed by the indigenous people in Peru were wrongly overlooked as unimportant, the consumption of which was only suitable for the lowest social classes.

The social role of women in agriculture was also changed forever. The Incas believed that women could work more intuitively with the Earth because their hearts were more open, but by imposing their new meat-eating habits, they adopted a scientific or "macho" approach.

I never developed an insatiable craving for the flesh of animals, but it was served to me at home for almost twenty-four years in a variety of forms, shapes, and styles. My mother used to stand at her post as a guard until the last piece of steak was gone from our plates. At that time, she used to tell us that we "needed" the flesh of animals in order to grow up stronger and healthier. Sometimes, it was very difficult to finish it all. I would wait for the littlest distraction on her part to wrap the pieces in a napkin and throw them under the dining room furniture to be picked up and thrown away in the middle of the night when everyone was sleeping. It was indeed a blessing when our first companion animals arrived to take care of that problem!

I also vividly remember the day my grandmother brought a chicken to the house. Innocently, I believed he was going to be a pet but, when he grew older and stronger, he was served to us for lunch. I refused to eat the bird and cried all night long. Maybe this was the first time that I rebelled against the consumption of meat. In my mind, I was unable to associate this living creature that spent lots of time with me with the dish that was served on the table. My first attempt at vegetarianism only lasted a short while. After a couple of weeks, I found myself justifying my meat-eating habits again. After all, the chickens I was eating were not the one we raised at home. In my limited mind, I was able to disassociate from the truth and the fact that cruelty and indifference cannot be separated just for our convenience.

During my college years, I met a classmate who always had problems during the lunch and dinner breaks. There was almost nothing for her to eat at the university cafeteria, and every time we met there we used to talk about the problems of being a vegetarian in a carnivorous society. Our conversations were mainly related to the health benefits of becoming a vegetarian. We never related to the sufferings animals have to endure to become food.

Shortly before I graduated as a translator, I became involved in a welfare group that mainly dealt with the problems associated with companion animal overpopulation. In order to educate the public, I used to devour all the educational materials that came from foreign countries. The materials that came in English and French were not as popular as the ones that came in Spanish, but I used to take them home with me to read on the weekends. Through these magazines, I learned what factory farms, downed animals, and battery cages were. Little by little, I started to associate old memories that were hidden somewhere in my mind— images of chickens being slaughtered in open markets, pigs' heads hanging from hooks, and large varieties of dead fish displayed in the counters of every supermarket in town. My most vivid memory was the noise the chickens made before they were killed. I remember I used to cover my ears every time this symphony of death filled the air of the open markets. Even though the cries were disturbing to me, I never asked where they came from, or, most importantly, why they were happening while no one paid any attention to them.

My mind quickly looked for another excuse. I wanted to believe that all those cruel pictures came from foreign countries and that the reality in Lima was quite different. I wanted to believe that farm animals in Peru lived happy lives in traditional roomy and ventilated farms and that, unfortunately, their destiny was to become food. I even wanted to believe they were killed humanely and quickly without unnecessary cruelty or torture. The pictures I saw in those magazines had to be the representation of a different reality, because my brain was unable to understand and accept the cruel and miserable conditions they had to endure.

I spent several weeks researching agricultural books and reports but could not find answers to all the questions I had. I looked at the situation from different points of view, trying to find a justification. From my parents I got factual answers based on the belief that we needed to eat animals to stay healthy; from my professors I got social and economic reasons to maintain a meat-based diet; and from the religious authorities I got the unequivocal excuse that animals were created by God to be consumed by people.

Unhappy with all my findings, I decided to look for answers myself and went to the local slaughterhouse. I have to admit that I never thought about what I was going to find there but, at the time, the idea seemed to be the only possible answer to all my questions. I was allowed to enter the facility with the excuse of writing a term paper about agricultural procedures. I was handed a pair of tall rubber boots and a plastic coat that I quickly put on without understanding the necessity of the attire. Later, I was going to fully understand why that equipment was needed.

I saw penned cows with labels hanging from their ears, walking in a circular motion towards their death. There were noises and a smell I had never smelled before. It was the stench of death that crossed the species barrier and sent chills down my spine. This was the first time in my entire life I had looked into the eyes of a cow. They were big, expressive, and gentle. Peaceful eyes looked back at me asking why we humans had to do this to them. I never felt more guilt in all my life. Those eyes were all the answers I needed. There was no need to continue with the visit, but I had to endure it to the end.

There were powerful reasons not to allow any cameras inside the slaughterhouse: pain, cruelty, flies, blood, intestines, smells of death, men with bloody tools killing conscious animals, and an unforgettable group of poor children searching in the trash containers for a piece of putrid meat.

I went back home and announced to my family that I wanted to be a vegetarian. Turmoil followed. I was lectured at endlessly about the multiple ways I was going to die. At the beginning, I was a little concerned about my family's premonitions because I was not educated about the great advantages of becoming a vegetarian. Nevertheless, I pretended I was absolutely ready to change. My father—being the tolerant and understanding human he has always been—kept an eloquent, but skeptical silence. He probably thought my news was just a new fad, another revolutionary idea to entertain my neverending search for new ideas and beliefs. After all, I had already been interested in becoming a Buddhist, a sociologist, an Egyptologist, and a radical animal liberator. He probably thought this new ideal was just going to fade away with time.

My mother, on the other hand, had a tougher approach. She told me quite clearly that she was not going to cook two different meals on a daily basis. Years later, she confessed that she just wanted to save my life by forcing me to maintain a meat-based diet.

My future was predicted and it was not a pretty picture: starvation, anemia, malnutrition, and eternal family conflict were my options. The struggle was difficult for a while, but I faced the obstacles with the strength that those bovine eyes in the slaughterhouses gave me the first time we looked at each other as two simple and equal creatures. I lived on pizzas and salads until I learned to loathe them, but persistence paid off in the end. My mother realized that my vegetarianism was not a simple novelty and started to cook vegetarian food just for me.

The ignorance of people, the conflicts at family functions, and the social isolation new vegetarians experience turned me into the most passionate champion of all the vegetarians on Earth. I wanted to change the world's meat-based diet overnight and at any price.

Now I realize how foolish I was every time I got into religious, health-related, or ethical arguments with people who were not ready to change. I remember the internal conflicts I experienced when I had to admit that I still loved people that were not on my side. I planned a variety of strategies and attacks, from appealing to the most sensible side of people to the use of the cruelest and crudest images to shock the incredulous. Nothing worked. Every hour, the world was still killing thousands of farm animals after a lifetime of confinement, immeasurable cruelty, and suffering caused by the taste preferences of the people.

It was after I became a vegan that I started to look at this phenomenon in a different way. I finally understood and accepted the fact that vegetarianism was a process of acquisition that happened at different levels and at different times. I also resigned myself to the fact that there was a possibility of vegetarianism not happening to some of the people who were very dear to me. I have to confess that on many occasions I secretly labeled some people as "incapable of changing," but destiny proved me wrong for the benefit of the animals.

Experience has improved my vision of a vegetarian/vegan world. And surprises knock at my door every day. A few months back, my parents, now in their seventies, became vegetarians. After my initial happiness, I wondered if it was too late for the health benefits to work. But, realizing that their change was a decision made with honesty and commitment, I decided just to be happy for the animals and for them. Hope may be slippery and ambivalent sometimes, but it does exist. After almost seventeen years of keeping a healthy and ethical diet, I have learned to patiently wait for those changes. But I do not wait in inactivity. I plant seeds and educate those who are willing to hear the message.

Many circumstances may trigger the enlightenment: a visit to a slaughterhouse, a book, a picture, a video, a second of reflection about what we do to sentient animals, a metaphor, a daughter living far away from you, or the idea of losing a child in the same brutal way farm animals lose their children. All of them are valid and powerful reasons to open our minds and hearts to those voiceless creatures that scream in agony in slaughterhouses.

A pair of eyes as beautiful and precious as the eyes of my three little daughters woke me up from the depths of my lethargic indifference. Those eyes are no longer present in this material reality, but I will never forget them, for they changed my entire life. Life was never fuller, richer, or more meaningful than it was at that moment. Those eyes told me that this fight was going to be long, hard, and difficult but it was going to be worth it. They told me that what is meant to be changed, always changes in due time.

These final thoughts are to my aging parents, who decided to embrace a new lifestyle. To my best friend, who never ate meat in front of me even before she became a vegetarian. To my girls, who had the wonderful opportunity to learn about compassion and respect for animals at a very early age. But most of all, these final thoughts are to that bovine friend and to all her kind. I heard her voice loud and clear and you could hear it, too.

❧ A Healthier, Happier Life ❧
PATRICK WEST

In 1996 I joined the Natural Law Party, a grassroots political party whose platform talked about bringing national life into harmony with natural law. After joining, reading the platform, and listening to different people speak, I began to realize the affects of my decisions and my lifestyle on the world around me. So I started to examine my lifestyle and the effects it had, which included taking a look at the way that I ate. I began reading books by John Robbins, specifically *Diet for a New America*. Reading this book, I realized that my meat-eating diet was having a significant impact on everything around me, from the inhumane treatment of animals to the deleterious effects on the environment. It was at this point that I decided to become a vegetarian, and then eventually a vegan.

There are so many reasons why I became a vegan. One reason was the effect that a non-vegan diet has on the animals. I tried to image what it would be like to be standing in line while just ahead of me my friends were being slaughtered. I tried to imagine what it would be like having my child taken away from me right after birth and kept in such horrible conditions, to be killed shortly thereafter.

Another reason I became a vegan was the negative effects of a meat- and dairy-based diet on my health, from the increased risk of cancer and heart disease to problems with my kidneys, liver, and intestines. But the health effects didn't stop there. I also had to consider the herbicides and pesticides used on the crops that are fed to animals that eventually cause health problems among humans, as well as the antibiotics and steroids in the animals that could affect my physiology and my immune system. Another reason I became a vegan was the environmental damage that the cattle industry, and factory farms in general, cause. I had to consider the decimation of the soil through erosion, causing desertification, as well as the amount of methane released by cattle and other animals, contributing to global warming. The list goes on and on.

Since becoming a vegetarian and then vegan, I have lost fifteen pounds, my cholesterol level dropped from 210 to 140, I have much more energy than before, and I feel good about myself. I feel good that I am making a difference in this world, just from the way that I eat.

It was toughest in the beginning, when I first became a vegetarian. Many people asked me the same old questions that I am sure most vegetarians have been asked. Where do you get your protein? Where do you get your calcium? Where do you get this nutrient, that nutrient, and the other? What do you eat, if it doesn't contain any animal products? And people couldn't understand why I would want to become a vegetarian. My wife is now a vegetarian, and we have raised our seventeen-month-old son without any dairy or meat. He is healthier than most other babies, has had fewer visits to the doctors, has a ton of energy, has been sick less often, and is in great spirits. We have done a lot of research on being vegetarians and we can now answer the questions with relative ease. We have found a lot of different cookbooks and have experimented with a great many different foods that we had never tried before. We even have our own traditions now for the holiday meals. It is still tough to go out to eat, trying to find places that carry vegetarian and vegan dishes, but we have managed. There are actually quite a lot of different restaurants that carry such choices. And, best of all, there are so many people that we have met along the way who are also vegetarians/vegans, and have become good friends with them.

All in all, I am extremely happy with the choice I have made. I have decided that I want to live a healthier, happier life, in harmony with the laws of nature, realizing what effects my lifestyle has on the world around me. And there are so many others who have come to the same realization. We do not own this planet and we have no implicit rights to use everything else in the world for our own benefit. We live in a world that is rich in the diversity of its species. We are just as much a part of nature as any other creature, and we need to take care of the environment around us. For when we take care of the environment around us, the environment around us will take care of us in turn.

❧ *My Journey to Vegetarianism* ❧
MICHELLE A. RIVERA

I was driving home from an animal-rights demonstration in January of 1988. I and my fellow activists had been to the circus to protest the use of animals at the "Cruelest Show On Earth." I was congratulating myself on how enlightened I was, how happy I was to have been a part of this demonstration, and how fulfilled I felt speaking out for the elephants, stallions, and tigers.

When I got home, I thought nothing of taking a couple of steaks out of the fridge and throwing them on the grill. Sitting down to dinner, my spouse casually remarked, "Don't you think this is just a little hypocritical? I mean, really, what is the difference between an elephant and a cow?" I looked into his deep brown eyes and told him that, yes, I knew that, but I didn't think that he, having been raised on meals that included meat every day, would sit still for going veggie. And that while I always wanted to, I couldn't bring myself to go veggie if I knew I had to still buy and cook meat for him and for our children. My husband assured me that he could give up red meat at home with no problem. That was the last time I ever ate red meat.

Giving up eating poultry came two years later when I went to work for The Animal Rights Foundation of Florida as assistant to their in-house counsel. It didn't take long for me to get with the program, surrounded by photos and videos and posters of factory-farm animals and battery hens. It was a very simple decision and I didn't feel that I was sacrificing at all. Quite the contrary, I was totally turned off by fowl and meat.

I had a problem giving up fish, however. I knew that Jesus was a fisherman, and I couldn't bring myself, a devout Catholic, to believe that He would have done anything wrong. But then, someone pointed out to me that dropping a hook in the water and pulling out one fish was a far cry from the commercial fishing of today. Today, we kill hundreds of thousands of species of marine life all in the name of fish dinners. If I could catch a fish myself, it wouldn't be quite as bad as contributing to the killing of all those marine animals. Of course, I could never bring myself to even consider killing a fish, and so giving up fish became surprisingly easy. After a while, it became second nature to me to give up dairy as well.

My rules for living this way are very simple. When I am at home, I eat like a vegan. I buy soy cheeses, butters, and soy milk. I don't eat eggs or stuff with eggs in it. But when I go out with my non-animal rights friends, or husband's partners (they're all lawyers), I play it cool. I order vegetarian food, of course, but don't put the server through the third degree about ingredients anymore. I never order soup, and I ask if the pasta is cooked in water or broth. But other than that, I pretty much stick to salads, breads, and pastas. I used to ask a lot of questions, but my husband just stopped taking me out with his friends, so, not liking the "banishment," I decided to lighten up a little. If we go to someone's home for dinner, I usually bring a veggie side dish, and I always try to bring transition foods, like Boca Burgers™ or the new buffalo wings from Morningstar Farms™, made with textured vegetable protein. Of course, I bring enough to share! Some of the fast food restaurants can be pretty accommodating, like the seven layer (hold the cheese) burrito from Taco Bell®, or the pasta bar at Wendy's™. But I only patronize those places if there is no other alternative; it is not something I do routinely. Going cruelty-free has been a long, involved process with several false starts. I don't buy or wear leather, but I sometimes still use honey in my tea. I know that bees are complicated creatures, and I have heard that they are killed for their honey, but I have also been told that they are only "smoked out," not burned out of their hives, so I guess the jury is still out on this one. I have more research to do. I also know that there are many who feed their companion animals vegetarian diets, and yet I can't bring myself to deprive my sweet dog and precious cat of the foods they so enjoy. So I am not quite there yet! Still some more things to aspire to. Guess I'm just a vegan wannabe!

One of the hardest, toughest challenges of going cruelty-free is the hidden ingredients. Finding out that Kodak™ uses animal products in their film but Fuji™ doesn't, or that certain jelly beans or gum drops have gelatin but others don't. I am constantly learning that there are new reasons to avoid certain products. Just recently, I went to my doctor for a flu shot and learned that the vaccine came from chickens. I couldn't do it. I had to leave without taking the shot. I learn something like this every day. The biggest challenge, I think, is wondering where it will all end.

I handle criticism very well. I know that this lifestyle isn't right for everyone, and I don't try to force my belief system on anyone. I would love it if the whole world went veggie, but I am also a big believer in "not judging lest you be judged" and I know that if I judge people harshly in this world, those standards will be used to judge me in the next. So I do what I know in my heart is right for me, and I hope that, someday, others will find it in their hearts to stop killing gentle animals.

❧ *A Hope for the Century* ❧
MICHELLE SCHREIBER

When I was in elementary school, my Gifted Education teacher passed around a basket with terribly boring, "big business" mini-project assignments in it. When the basket came my way, there were only two assignments left to choose from: the New York Stock Exchange or Factory Farming. Neither appealed to me, but imagining that learning about cows standing in green pastures and tractors had to be more interesting than having to do research in the *Wall Street Journal*, I chose Factory Farming.

I already knew that the meat on my dinner plate was actually parts of my animal friends. For years, I had been driving my parents crazy at suppertime by refusing to finish my meal after pulling odd bits out of my hamburger and imagining that I could tell that this piece used to be a ligament, and that one a bone. Upon identifying hot dogs as a ground-up pig, the thought of actually consuming one turned my stomach. My grandmother once served chicken still attached to the bone at a picnic, and when I was given a leg to eat, I ran inside the house crying and refused to eat anything all day. Thus, my parents were none too surprised when literature depicting what really happens on factory farms arrived in the mail for my report and, after reading it, I promptly announced that I was now a vegetarian.

Of all of the anti-factory farming books, brochures, and fact-sheets that I researched for my report, the story that set in stone my life's path of fighting for animals was one I wrote myself as part of my project. Through writing it, I realized that animals—even those who weren't the family dog—have emotions, and can feel pain just as we do. My story followed a piglet from the moment of his birth to the moment of his death in a factory farm. There was no grass, no sunlight, and no mud for him—just cold cement and fluorescent lights. I remember looking up through my tears at my classmates' open mouths after I read them my story of the pig crying as his mother was taken to her death, how his tail was chopped off, how insanely bored he grew locked in a tiny stall, his cries of pain after his horrifying ride in the transport truck as his skin frozen to the side of the truck was ripped from his body, and his screams of terror as he was hung upside down and his neck sliced open. After hearing that story, not one of my classmates ever teased me about being a vegetarian.

A few years later, I attended a vegetarian conference at which People for the Ethical Treatment of Animals (PETA) was tabling. I picked up some literature, and this time, reading it with a mind more mature than that of an elementary student's, became a vegan. My mother thought I would be dead within the year from malnutrition, but here I am, with more than fifteen years of being vegan under my belt, at the age of twenty-seven, grateful to my compassionate diet for keeping me healthy and helping me avoid the seemingly hereditary cholesterol and weight problems of my family. Now my mother telephones me each day she eats vegetarian just to share the news.

It is completely beyond my comprehension that someone could think it is all right to strap down an elephant and beat her, or shove chemicals in rabbits' eyes. When I was a child, I believed that if I opened the skulls of animal abusers and scooped out the part of their brain that apparently was rotten mush, they would suddenly become sensible and start volunteering at their local SPCA. Unfortunately, it is not that simple.

Education, I have discovered, is the key. Thanks to PETA's efforts to educate the public, the USDA is pushing for more soy and less meat in our children's school lunches, the then Vice President of the United States, Al Gore, saved the lives of more than 800,000 animals by halting massive tests on chemicals until cruelty-free testing methods are developed for the program, and a global outcry helped fourteen baby elephants, some still of nursing age, who were stolen from their families in the wild to be sold to circuses or zoos, find their way back to freedom. Students are calling our dissection hotline for help in their refusal to cut open frogs. Letters that begin, "Thank you for opening my eyes..." or "I had no idea they did that to chickens until I read your article..." pour into our office—all testimonials from people who have stopped wearing fur, leather, and wool, or eating animals after learning what really happens. People are learning. Even my fiancé, whose father was a grantmaker to vivisectors, and whose grandfather was a dairy farmer, now believes that dogs belong inside with their adopted human families rather than chained outside, scours the ingredients list on food packages at the grocery store to make sure it's vegan, and refuses to buy anything from Procter & Gamble because the company tests its products on animals.

My fiancé used to complain that I'm always at work and am never home. "Do you really have to check your voice mail messages again?" he used to ask. He doesn't anymore, now that he understands that working for the animals isn't a nine to five job. Things won't change if someone doesn't go the extra mile. Someone needs to comfort the dog who's been abandoned, give peace to the cow who's been tortured, help prosecute the boys who burned and mutilated a cat, hear the shouts of the orangutans being beaten and go after the abuser, hear the pigs scream, stop the monkeys from going insane in their tiny cages, save the kittens from cruel experiments, draw attention to the horse who collapsed in the walk from the circus train to the ring, end the pit bull fights, close down the fur farms, end hunting, and find new alternative testing methods. The tales of torture pour into our office—the boy who microwaved a cat, the tiger who decided he had been punched in the head one too many times and bit off the arm of his trainer and was then shot to death in his cage, the mayor who kicks a dog to death. Someone has to pay attention to the suffering. One of those someones is me.

My hope is that when you read this piece a hundred years from now, you will have never seen a performing elephant, never adorned yourself with an animal's skin, never suffered from a disease whose cure was delayed by barbaric animal tests, and never tasted the flesh of an animal. My wish is that, by your generation, it will finally be recognized that animals have the right to live their lives as individuals, and not as objects to be used. Just as the oppression of African Americans and women is now looked back upon as shocking and simple minded, I believe that in a century's time, animal cruelty will be a thing of the past.

❧ *The Sounds of the Knives* ❧

REBEKAH HARP

Although I've always thought of myself as a person who was compassionate towards all animals, it was not until a few years ago that I took an ethical stand against the practice of eating meat. In other words, I finally put my morals where my mouth was. I was raised by carnivorous parents, in a home where, in fact, having meat on the dinner table was a sign of prosperity. There was a time that steak was my favorite meal.

However, now the image of a cow carcass on my plate is enough to elicit a wave of nausea. For some reason, for years I was able to separate my feelings for "non-food" animals from those who in our culture have been unlucky enough to exist for our consumption. I would proudly proclaim that "Fur is Dead" or link arms with other advocates in protest at animal abuse or experimentation; but I would not hesitate at all as I bit into a hamburger.

Then it happened.

I was enjoying a steak dinner at a nice restaurant, and I looked around at the people in the room. When I recall the event, I always remember it in slow motion, like a scene from an Oliver Stone film. The sounds of the knives sawing through the slabs of cow became magnified, and the rivulets of blood and grease pooling on the plates made me sick. An image of terrified cows awaiting their slaughter flashed through my mind—and that was the last animal I ever ate. Those cows were no different from my dogs or cats, so how could I continue to justify eating any animal?

My becoming a vegetarian was a process of enlightenment. That's how I feel most people are—compassionate people who, for whatever reason, have simply not been enlightened in regard to mankind's relationship with animals. One of the most incredible by-products of my vegetarian lifestyle is that the weight of hypocrisy has been lifted from my shoulders. I am no longer haunted by a visual flash of a pig's face while stuffing my face with a sausage biscuit. The meat department at the grocery store now closely resembles something from the set of a horror movie. I am nauseated by the smell of animal flesh grilling at a barbecue.

Yet I am comforted by the fact that I am part of a growing population of different thinkers, part of a renaissance of a new, compassionate human species. After many years of eating animals, it is sometimes a bit strange to me that I don't miss eating meat at all anymore. I feel empowered by my freedom of choice—content in knowing that I am no longer responsible for the slaughter of defenseless animals.

Now, when I look into an animal's eyes, I feel pure joy, not guilt. As I do so, the cost of my liberation ceases to exist.

❧ Why I Am a Vegetarian ❧
RICHARD H. SCHWARTZ, PH.D.

Until about 1977, I was a meat-and-potatoes person. My mother was sure to prepare my favorite dish—pot roast—whenever I came to visit with my wife and children. It was a family tradition that I would be served a turkey drumstick every Thanksgiving. Yet, not only have I become a vegetarian, but I also now devote a major part of my time to writing, speaking, and teaching about the benefits of vegetarianism. What caused this drastic change?

In 1975, I began teaching a course, "Mathematics and the Environment," at the College of Staten Island. The course uses basic mathematical concepts and problems to explore current critical issues, such as pollution, resource scarcities, hunger, energy, and the arms race. While reviewing material related to world hunger, I became aware of the tremendous waste of grain associated with the production of beef. (Over seventy percent of the grain produced in the United States is fed to animals destined for slaughter, while an estimated twenty million of the world's people die annually due to hunger and its effects.) In spite of my own eating habits, I often led class discussions on the possibility of reducing meat consumption as a way of helping hungry people. After several semesters of this, I took my own advice and gave up eating red meat, while continuing to eat chicken and fish.

I then began to read about the many health benefits of vegetarianism and about the horrible conditions for animals raised on factory farms. I was increasingly attracted to vegetarianism, and on January 1, 1978, I decided to join the International Jewish Vegetarian Society. I had two choices for membership: (1) practicing vegetarian (one who refrains from eating any flesh); (2) non-vegetarian (one who is in sympathy with the movement, while not yet a vegetarian). I decided to become a full practicing vegetarian, and since then have avoided eating any meat, fowl, or fish.

Since that decision, I have learned much about vegetarianism's connections to health, nutrition, ecology, resource usage, hunger, and the treatment of animals. I also started investigating connections between vegetarianism and Judaism. I learned that the first Biblical dietary law (Genesis 1:29) was strictly vegetarian, and I became convinced that important Jewish mandates to preserve our health, be kind to animals, protect the environment, conserve resources, share with hungry people, and seek and pursue peace all pointed to vegetarianism as the best diet for Jews (and everyone else) today. To get this message to a wider audience I wrote a book, *Judaism and Vegetarianism*, which was published in 1982. (A second expanded edition was published in 1988, and a newly revised edition in 2001.)

Increasingly, I have come to see vegetarianism as not only a personal choice, but also a societal imperative, an essential component in the solution of many national and global problems. The U. S. Surgeon General has indicated that sixty-eight percent of diseases in the United States are related to poor diets, and this is a major factor behind the major changes that have occurred in the U.S. health care system. Also, modern intensive animal-based agriculture is a major contributor to many current environmental and public health threats, such as the destruction of tropical rain forests and other habitats, global warming, soil erosion and depletion, water shortages, air and water pollution, the proliferation of antibiotic-resistant, and disease-causing bacteria.

I have recently been spending more and more time trying to make others aware of the importance of switching toward vegetarian diets, for them and for the world. I have: appeared on over sixty radio and cable television programs; had many letters and several op-ed articles in the *Staten Island Advance* and other publications; spoken frequently at the College of Staten Island and to community groups; given many talks and met with three chief rabbis and other religious and political leaders in Israel, while visiting my two daughters and their families in the last few years. I started a "Campaign for a Vegetarian-Conscious Israel by 2000." I was selected as the "Jewish Vegetarian of the Year" by the Jewish Vegetarians of North America in 1987. I now have over a hundred articles on the Internet at arrs.envirolink.org/ar-voices/schwartz/, and am working with others at setting up a comprehensive Jewish vegetarian web site.

I have always felt good about my decision to become a vegetarian. Putting principles and values into practice is far more valuable and rewarding than hours of preaching. When people ask me why I gave up meat, I welcome the opportunity to explain the many benefits of vegetarianism.

While my family was initially skeptical about my change of diet, they have become increasingly understanding and supportive. In 1993, my younger daughter was married in Jerusalem at a completely vegetarian wedding.

Recently, I have noted some signs of increased interest in vegetarianism, and many people are concerned about dietary connections to health, nutrition, animal rights, and ecology. Yet, McDonald's is rapidly expanding in many countries, including Israel, China, and Russia. So there is much that still needs to be done. My hope is to be able to keep learning, writing, and speaking about vegetarianism, to help bring closer that day when, in the words of the motto of the International Jewish Vegetarian Society, ". . . no one shall hurt nor destroy in all of God's holy mountain" (Isaiah 11.9).

❧ *Our Vegetarian Family* ❧
ROCHELLE MITCHELL

I stopped eating red meat while I was pregnant with my second child. I had an aversion to the smell, taste, and sight of bloody red flesh, to everything about it. After my baby was born, I didn't go back to it. I still ate fish and poultry.

About a year later, my twin sister became a vegetarian and told me the benefits of a vegetarian diet. She also introduced me to *Stop the Insanity* by Susan Powter. I lost fifteen pounds by exercising and eating low-fat food. I prepared vegetarian meals for my family several times a week (beans are lower in fat than chicken). However, my husband would sneak off to get his chicken nuggets after every meatless meal, claiming he needed his meat to feel full. By this time, we were eating vegetarian meals three or four times a week. I suggested we go vegetarian completely since we were almost there, but my husband wouldn't hear of it. He said it was impossible. He had been vegetarian several times before and it had never lasted. He was always drawn back to eating meat.

Then one day, my husband heard a radio show about the benefits of a vegetarian diet and how the cattle industry fools us into eating meat. He wanted to go vegetarian that night. The next day, I gave my cans of tuna to a friend, ate one last chicken sandwich, and never looked back.

We didn't force our diet on our daughter who was two at the time. We continued to allow her to go to McDonald's. We explained to her that the chicken nuggets she was eating used to be a chicken that went "cluck-cluck." She didn't believe us. After she made that connection, she gave up her chicken nuggets. She now won't step foot in a McDonald's. She's more militant about vegetarianism than I am. Now my whole family is vegetarian, including our new baby, who has never eaten meat in her life.

❧ *Through My Children's Eyes* ❧
TAMMY

This is the story of how my children and I became vegetarians. One day as I was sitting at the computer looking at the website of People for the Ethical Treatment of Animals (www.peta.org), my daughter Ashlee (aged six) came up to me and said, "Mom, what's that?" I began to describe exactly what the site was—how the organization thought people should be vegetarians so animals didn't have to die. We looked at the site together and decided that we would try and become vegetarians for the animals. We went shopping and looked at what was out there for vegetarians. I explained to my children that they would have to sacrifice a lot, like McDonald's, jello, marshmallows, some candy, and much more. They didn't even have to think about it: "Mom we will do it for the animals so they don't have to suffer." So we started making the transition. As of December 1, 1998 we have given up all meat and any products that have been tested on animals. We will not wear anything that contains animal by-products, such as leather.

My children sometimes feel the sacrifice when playing with other kids that get to go to all the fast food restaurants, but they never question what they have done. What they do question is why everyone doesn't become a vegetarian to save the animals. We drive by the cow pastures and they say, "Mommy, if everyone stopped eating meat these cows wouldn't have to die." I try and explain to them that, while we can't make everyone give up eating meat, by us doing it we have not only saved the lives of thousands of animals but we have saved rain forests and we have also saved the Earth from added stress.

The thing that amazes most people is that my children made the choice; I did not make them. They decided to do it on their own. Most adults can't make that sacrifice, and that is why they try and justify their eating of animals and have a hard time understanding why we do what we do.

The harshest criticism we encounter is from our own family. Family members seem to be so concerned that we are not getting enough protein or enough vitamins. It's funny, but I am concerned for them on the same issues. I am amazed that I lived as long as I did eating things that were so unhealthy for me. I thank goodness my kids were wise enough to get us all to change. Hopefully, I can do right by all my years of eating meat.

Eating out is harder and harder to do. For some reason people see it as a joke when you tell them you don't eat meat. I have a tendency not to say I am vegetarian because I have a feeling they want to make a fool of me. Maybe I am overly worried about it, but having seen the looks on people's faces when they hear I am vegetarian, it makes me realize that I must be careful with the words I use.

I think the best defense when people ask me why I am vegetarian is to let my children explain it. Opponents never seem to have an argument for the children. And how could they, when a seven-year-old says, "How can *you* eat dead animals? I don't want animals to suffer just so I can eat, when I can eat things so they don't suffer. Animals have feelings too, you know. Animals shouldn't have to die just so we can eat. Have you ever tried veggie nuggets? No animals had to die and they taste good!"

❧ *Why I Chose a Vegetarian Life* ❧
TOM GALLAGHER

The first time I tried to stop eating meat, I was fourteen and made it about three weeks. The second time I tried to quit the meat diet I was fifteen. I thought it was for health reasons. I'd been reading books for support, which helped a lot (since I knew no one close who was a vegetarian). One book advocated a "gradual" health-rationale approach (which I adopted)—quit each type of flesh food in order of unhealthiness—first pig, then cow, then bird, then fish, then egg/diary. I went through all, quitting all but fish in less than a week, eating fish less and less until about ten years later, when I just couldn't force my self to eat fishes anymore, even once a year! So I was a "near-vegetarian" to that point.

After leaving the fishes alone, I was then a "vegetarian" or "lacto-ovo vegetarian" (someone who eats milk and eggs, but no animal food that was ever alive and then killed for human food). This I still am.

Now at age forty, twenty-five years later, I'm experimenting with veganism. I haven't had an egg in years (can't stand 'em anymore!) but still use milk in coffee and in pre-made foods. Lately, I've realized it's nice to have "support" from other vegetarian people—support against the pressure of the majority culture that doesn't understand our choice. Also, I've come to realize that when I became a vegetarian—even though it was easier then to think I wanted to change for "health reasons"—I did so not really knowing why I wanted to do it, but just knowing I did want to!

I think my choice was, as it remains, based on ethics and aesthetics. Why should I kill for food when it's not necessary? And killing without good reason is ugly! I feel good and powerful not killing. I feel beautiful not killing. The health reason is certainly there—I feel quite healthy indeed! But at my stage in this way of living, I attribute my motivation (other than inertia!) to ethics and aesthetics.

For a lacto-ovo vegetarian, dining out is easy, especially after twenty-five years of practice and twenty-five years of gradual social change for the better. Vegan choices also seem more plentiful, at least here in Minneapolis. There are many restaurants that are vegetarian-friendly, and a few that are all or mostly vegetarian. I try to support only vegetarian-friendly restaurants, both as a matter of personal convenience and as an agent of social change.

Rarely do I hear outright negative comments about my being vegetarian. The most common, uncomfortable moment is while eating a meal with flesh-eating people in a public place. I inquire of the wait staff about vegetarian options, ingredients, etc., they overhear, and good-naturedly offer: "Oh, you're vegetarian. Why do you do it?" as they are swallowing some flesh-food. "What can I say," I think to myself. If I tell them why, while they are eating animal meat, there will be discomfort for both or all of us. Usually, I say I don't like to discuss it at meals, for obvious reasons. Generally, my questioners pause a moment and accept that. If they push it further, I'll disclose that at first it was for health reasons, but now it's for ethical and aesthetic reasons. Once in a while, we really get into a debate. I find that people tend to be more defensive about this topic when they are engaged in the act of eating animal flesh. I feel great compassion for meat-eaters, since I believe this is what they were taught by the majority culture, even though it is wrong in my view.

Are vegans better than lacto-ovo vegetarians? After being a lacto-ovo vegetarian for a couple of decades, I've seen people who have adopted the macrobiotic and vegan diets, which I respect, look down at my lacto-ovo vegetarianism. Then, a year later, I see them eating flesh food! They only made it a month, a year, or three years. I believe that the Buddhists, who say "follow the Middle Way," may be on to something. Perseverance furthers. I think that it is better to be lacto-ovo vegetarian for a long time than a vegan for a week or a year. After a long time as a lacto-ovo vegetarian, it is easier to go vegan more often or completely, later.

I think we need to develop more of a connected culture among vegetarians, for mutual support as well as outreach to those who will join us.

A Puddle of Blood

JEFF LYDON

On a school night in the winter of my tenth year, already two hours past dark, we were ready to have dinner. In my family, an expensive cut of beef didn't mark any special occasion. The grocery store was the one place my mother refused to cut corners. We had the best steak, chicken, roast beef, ham, bacon, turkey, eggs, and fish money could buy, and we washed it down with a tall glass of milk. Of course, in 1979, the negative effects of meat-eating were a better kept secret than they are now.

I was hungry. Steak was on the menu. We sat in ladder-back chairs around an antique American table, much too big for just the four of us. There were the potatoes, a basket of bread, and too close was a bowl of overcooked string beans, my portion of which I would later hide in a napkin when my parents weren't looking. The main course arrived on a blue serving platter. My mother set it next to me. I remember the old oven mitts she wore, stained and worn so thin that she burned her hands more nights than not.

She told me to dig in. My father waited his turn. I stabbed the biggest cut. The juice ran out from the slightly charred slab and filled the grooves in the plate. I stopped with the serving fork deep in meat. My father waited.

An innocent question from a child, perhaps even stupid from a ten-year-old, like asking why the snow is white. But I didn't ask about the snow. I asked why the juice was red. Before the question had finished its short journey out of my mouth, the answer came in one word like harsh light into sleep: blood. The juice is red because the juice is blood.

My father told me to stop playing. I put the thing on my plate and ate it, blood and all.

That was a few years before I became the only vegetarian in my school, earning myself the nickname Buddha. And well before that night, I had learned to love animals and to dread their persecution. (In elementary school, I'd raised money for Greenpeace to save the whales, about the same time my future wife, Sarah, living just across town, was writing letters to her representative about the slaughter of seals.) But the night when I saw the juice for what it was was probably the first time I connected the flesh and blood I was chewing to the neighbor's cows, to the butchered whales, to my German Shepherd, to the pain I knew whenever I saw my own blood.

Twenty years later, in the autumn of 1999, my mother came to see Sarah and me in our small, rented home on the outskirts of Ithaca, New York, not far from Farm Sanctuary. By now, her oven mitts long gone, she'd reached her seventy-first year to see four of her five children grow into vegetarians. In spite of how much we talked to her about how eating meat ravages our bodies, our environment, and the animals, she had clung to a bit of myth that has probably killed a lot of people: anything in moderation is all right. Sarah and I took my mother to Farm Sanctuary, where the two of us had visited and volunteered often. For the first time in her life, my mother petted a pig, and was gently nuzzled by an 800-pound cow named Penelope, whose nose was bigger than my mother's head.

My mother has always been a dog-lover. Now she lives in an apartment where she can't have a dog. That cow and that pig reached her the way a dog does; she crossed the bridge between heart and head to find no difference between eating Penelope and eating one of her beloved dogs. I know this because the next day, after she'd returned to her apartment two hours north of Ithaca, my mother called to say she had decided to stop eating meat.

❧ A Field of Grazing Cows ❧
JENNIE TAYLOR MARTIN

I grew up loving animals and finding them to be much better company than humans. Being the youngest of seven kids, I was lucky that my family was very supportive of my "eccentric" nature. Their support made me feel "special" about the way I felt about animals.

For as far back as I can remember, I had always made it a point to visit all of the dogs who lived in my neighborhood. My mom was terrified of strange dogs, so you can imagine the look on her face the day a Great Dane friend decided to come over for a visit. I'm sure he felt he was just coming by to see me in the same way that I came by to see him. My mom insisted that I take him home, but she did allow me to sit with him on our front porch first (even at that young age, I felt that he wouldn't understand why I was running him home after he'd come all that way for a visit). My connection to animals wasn't just limited to the cute and cuddly type either. I once befriended a spider who was living in our bathroom. Unfortunately, my father didn't know he was a "friend" until after he'd done the awful deed of killing him. Bugs in our house were never killed so nonchalantly again!

When I reached my twenties, I became aware of the book *Diet for a New America* and had the opportunity to attend a talk given by the author, John Robbins. At that time, and in my earlier growing years, I never ate meat that looked like it came from an animal (e.g., steak), but I still hadn't gotten the connection and was eating the typical American diet. This book gave me that connection. Even though I cried as I read it, I didn't yet take that final step. It was shortly after reading that book that I was driving down a country road in Chesapeake, Virginia, when I passed a field with grazing cows. I looked over at them and thought, "You don't have to worry about me, I would never hurt you." And that's when it happened—I became vegetarian. I have never looked back or had any regrets about my vegetarianism. I feel even closer to animals today than I did as a child, because now I have a clear conscience!

❧ Going Veggie ❧
JOHANNA MCCLOY

People often ask me when I became a vegetarian, and why. They wonder if there was a specific event that triggered the decision, or perhaps a person. There were many. As I see it, however, I was born a vegetarian. It's just that I was living in a meat-eating family, and I didn't know that I really had a choice. It's like the layers of ignorance were slowly shed until the real me was revealed.

Dinner in my home consisted of the standard meat staple, a handful of vegetables and perhaps a baked potato. I grew up overseas, in a number of different countries, which made buying fresh and inexpensive produce a practical impossibility. For us, vegetables, for the most part, came in a can. We lived in New Delhi for a number of years when I was seven years old, and I remember that even the meat selection was dismal. When my mother complained about having to eat water buffalo, that might've been the first time anything registered for me. Water buffalo. This was an animal I could picture. A wild animal. Not a meat product found in the refrigerated section of your local market. It bothered me when it was served, and the ongoing dialogue, comparing it to other meats, only fueled this new awareness.

The other factor that contributed to this awareness was all the cows that roamed free outside our house there. Hindu belief is that cows are sacred. Not to be eaten. Again, the realization would hit me: Meat Equals Animals. Real animals. I continued to eat meat, but I was only comfortable as long as I didn't see it being prepared. I didn't like looking at the packages in the store and I *really* couldn't stand handling it in its raw form. It disgusted me so much that I literally felt nauseated.

I remember one afternoon, when my mother asked me to rinse the chicken under the sink and prepare it for cooking. Seeing the blood made me start crying. And touching it made everything inside me feel *wrong wrong wrong*. I was young and I was sheltered from any other way of life, so I thought my sensitivity needed to be disguised. Other people didn't seem to react this way. Something had to be wrong with me. I made a few remarks about the horror of seeing the blood and handling the raw skin, but this only triggered a little laughter. Laughter at my lack of awareness. Laughter that told me, you'll get over it. But I didn't.

California played a big part in my shift toward vegetarianism. We went to California on summer vacations and vegetables there were luxuriously tasty and abundant and cheap. We ate lots of salads and fresh, steamed vegetables with dinner, making this portion of the meal a special and valued treat. Garden sandwiches were typically on a lunch menu and I loved them: avocado, tomato, cheese and sprouts. Not a hint of meat to be found anywhere. Finally, while attending college, I started to make the bigger shift toward vegetarianism. My boyfriend was a food coop member and an avid cook, eager to try any new recipe that consisted of yet another alternative meat staple, such as a grain or falafel. We still ate chicken or fish, but my appetite for healthier and natural foods grew very quickly.

My progression toward a vegetarian diet paralleled my sensitivity to animals in general. I was averse to seeing them perform in any way. I was very keenly aware of abusive treatment to animals known as pets. I even volunteered to assist the neighborhood's veterinarian when we lived in Tokyo. Even though we could barely communicate, I found myself drawn to this place, this place that *cared* for animals.

I was bothered more and more by meat. I was thinking more and more about stopping and becoming a vegetarian. I now saw that this was a reasonable option by meeting others who'd made that choice. Finally, one day in 1988, I was driving the long and boring stretch of the I-5 between Sacramento and Los Angeles in California. I got behind a truck filled with chickens. Live chickens in cages. Feathers flying out and hitting my windshield. I couldn't take it. I tried to pass, but this truck kept meeting me every so often, for *hours*, until I knew I couldn't eat this stuff ever again. I passed Butterfield Ranch and found myself feeling like I was in hell. Endless pastures of cattle to my right, and a chicken truck in front of me. I vowed right there and then that I would never eat meat again. So far so good. No more red meat. No more chicken.

Fish? I didn't grow up eating fish. Fish wasn't a part of our diet for some reason. If we ever ate it, I associated fish with scales and fishy smells. I declared my aversion for it on those grounds and never ate it. Tuna, however, was another story. That wasn't fish. And fish wasn't meat. I didn't make that connection for a *long* time. I had no exposure to fish. I only started to eat it and find it tasty after I stopped eating other meats. Salmon, halibut, or swordfish would be my dinner selections at restaurants. my source for protein. People started to ask me, "Why is fish okay?" I didn't have a good answer. At first, I tried to come up with one, but after a while, I couldn't deliver it, so I copped to the fact that this was an obvious contradiction. I knew the day would come when I would stop eating this, too.

I have recently passed my first year anniversary since I stopped eating fish, and thus meat altogether. It feels great. I've taken to tofu and I eat exactly the way I want to. There are no contradictions in my diet anymore and I feel really, really good about that. I am finding protein alternatives that I enjoy and have collected a pile of recipes that I intend to try in the years to come. I feel wonderful. I feel like I'm coming out of a shell and owning my real self. The voice within is no longer silent. It is the voice I use. It is audible. It is who I am inside and out.

In the process of owning my beliefs and living in accordance with them, I have encountered my fair share of conflicts and awkward situations. Whether it be dinner at someone's home where meat is the entrée; or finding myself at a venue where no meat alternatives exist; or disappointing the people around me by requiring special treatment...it is this shift toward being true to myself that has also spurred a demand for self assertiveness and composure. I struggled with it for a while, still feeling shame or guilt for putting people in awkward or self-conscious situations. I tried to find a way to be tactful, to be diplomatic, and not to push my beliefs on anyone. Living by example. This was my credo. I wasn't about to impose my views.

This, too, has shifted. I've become more vocal about animal rights and humane animal treatment over the years and I now have a difficult time holding back those feelings when they are prodded by someone's ignorance or their decision to continue being in denial. I'm amazed by that.

The little voice inside is now taking over. I'm coming out of my cocoon. It doesn't make me the most popular girl on the block and I'm more than fine with that, which is a big part of the process. I stand by my convictions. The more I learn about the negligent treatment of animals across the globe, the more I'm compelled to be their voice and to take action to change things. I try to be tactful, to be appropriate to the circumstances, to deliver information with love and compassion. I know there's only so much I can control or change in the here and now.

I will try to continue being an example by being true to myself. I give voice to my beliefs and I take particular care to show children that they have a choice, too. I didn't have anyone as an example when I grew up. I didn't have a mirror for my own beliefs. I felt like perhaps I was too sensitive, that my beliefs made me different and weird. I don't want other kids to feel that way.

I buy cruelty-free products. I buy leather alternatives. I buy products without animal ingredients. I speak for animals that are abused or neglected around the world. I feel good about these things. And I'm glad if I can be an example to just one kid or adult.

It's been eleven years since I ate poultry or red meat, one year since I ate fish. I might stop eating eggs soon. Perhaps dairy will follow. I don't know. For now, I feel like I'm making a difference—for myself, primarily, but hopefully also for all the people around me who see that it's not only possible to make this choice, but also to love it.

❧ Quiet Determination ❧
KAREN MOSS

I'm almost forty years old and I guess that I made the decision to become a vegetarian when I was seventeen and working in a health food store.

I was a typical teen sneaking treats from the fruit carts in the back. After about one month of this, I discovered a marked improvement in a chronic stomach ailment that had haunted me all my life. I also noted that I just felt better, with more energy, etc. I began to read the book *Lead, Kindly Light* by Vincent Sheean about the life of Mahatma Gandhi and began paying attention to other important people who had made the decision to become vegetarian for moral and ethical reasons.

I was science-oriented, and Frances Moore Lappé's book *Diet for a Small Planet* provided me with so many indisputable facts and figures that I could no longer lead my life eating animals. It was an evolution for me to become a vegetarian. I always remember this when speaking to those that would harass me for it. I have to withhold anger and treat them with the gentle kindness of one who only offers them a simple truth: that animals were not put on Earth for us and that we are part of the animal world, not the sovereign leader of it.

I have endured incredible resistance for my lifestyle, as any vegetarian would attest. I worked in a male-dominated profession in the South, where the Sunday barbecue is attended with an almost religious fervor. Those who would oppose me could never keep their tongues silent as I heaped on the potato salad and bypassed the burgers. Whenever I have been confronted, I have always tried to keep a calm, resistant disposition as I counted out the reasons for my eating habits. This seems to unnerve even the most aggressive haranguers. As Gandhi knew, quiet determination will eventually erode the most cruel and assertive of our kind.

I hope that vegetarians will continue to grow in number. It is such a relief to eat without guilt or doubt. It takes a lot of courage to take an unwavering look at the cruelty involved in a non-vegetarian diet. To face the staggering facts of the business of turning animals into meals one must endure the deepest and most penetrating pain of realization. I really believe this is why many people are not vegetarians. They will not take that turn in the road to gaze upon humankind's atrocities. Many of my friends will tell me, "Please, that's enough, I don't want to hear anymore," when I try to tell them about an animal cruelty.

To all the other vegetarians who like me took the other fork in the road and live every day with the sadness that is part of knowing the truth, I say "Hooray to you!" Your pain comes out of growth and your growth is part of our eventual evolution to become a kinder species.

Environmental Wacko

KEITH M. FOLINO

I'm a wacko: a minimal-consuming, animal-loving, tree-saving, recycling, ozone-protecting, population-squelching, vegetarian of the worst kind. I know this, and I rue the day that my mind started to go.

It didn't happen all at once. I can remember walking across a busy downtown street in Cleveland, Ohio long before the move to clean up Lake Erie had begun. Randy Newman had not yet sung his now-famous lyric—"burn on big river, burn on." Slave to a powerful nicotine-jones, I dodged impatient traffic and stripped cellophane from the top of a new pack of Camel regulars. I peeled back the tin foil and threw the small crumpled wad onto the sidewalk as I hopped up onto the curb.

There's no telling what triggers an "Earth Day" virus. Mine lay insidiously dormant in my heart for years before swimming slowly along my veins into the gray matter between my ears. But once the parasite awoke, there was no stopping its invasive effect. I watched that little ball of foil and plastic bounce along the sidewalk before rolling into the gutter beside a pile of litter, and the initial symptom of my disease reared its ugly head. A small light flashed behind my eyes, and I heard a whisper, the first in a neverending torrent of manic musings: "You live on this planet, Keith. Why would you want to trash it up?"

Now, years later, smart people do everything they can to avoid letting my disease contaminate their minds. They know I'm beyond hope. They smile condescendingly, as I banter about the need for them to separate their aluminum cans from their trash or the likelihood that the chicken they are preparing for their family is besieged with E-coli or salmonella.

I must be deranged! Why else would such awful thoughts course through my mind? The stench of cramped warehouses lighted seventeen hours a day. Cages stacked high from end to end, the sorry tenants, beaks seared off at birth, defecating on those below, while their feet become one with the wire floor. Seven weeks later their unnaturally plumped bodies skewered end-to-end bleeding the prized flesh that saner members of our society wait impatiently to devour in box restaurants lining the roads across our nation.

Normal people aren't troubled by what lies under the special sauce between their sesame-seed buns either. They crowd beneath the golden arches, wolfing down their food while wackos like me wonder how many acres of rain forest disappeared to provide those "billions and billions" of burgers. Why, I wonder, doesn't heating meat to a temperature calculated to kill the bacteria in it seem like a reasonable solution to me? I'm goofy! That's the only possible explanation. Hell, I'm so off-balance I wouldn't only try to stop a friend from eating this fecal fare, I'd push him aside if he were getting ready to step in it.

I hear voices (more proof that I'm wacko) whispering terrible things to me! The Earth's population has doubled in twenty years while nearly a billion people are starving, and most of our grain is fed to livestock. It takes seven pounds of precious grain and 2,464 gallons of water to produce one pound of beef. Fifty-five square feet of rain forest is slashed and burned for every quarter pound burger imported from that region. Twenty-five percent of the Central and South American rain forest has disappeared since 1960. The number one non-point source of pollution in North America comes from livestock waste and the pesticides and fertilizers used to grow feed. Inside my disturbed dome, this kind of logic just doesn't add up.

Oh, I've tried to get normal over the years. I would hide from the other loonies every once in a while. I'd find a quiet place by myself and I would eat meat. But the last time that happened, I couldn't stop thinking about where the ribs exposed on my plate had come from. I smothered them with the thick sauce coagulating in a little white paper cup beside my plate and fought off a nagging vision of similar ribs stretched over the taught skin of some starving child in sub-Saharan Africa. I tried not to dwell on the feeling that my veins were filling with a yellow, gelatinous glycerin.

I worked hard to retrieve my sanity, but in the end, I knew I was still completely wacko. I pushed the plate of bones and gristle away, tongued a stringy piece of pig-flesh wedged between my molars, and listened to the whisper of voices at the back of my mind again: "It's your mouth Keith. Why would you want to trash it up?"

❧ *An Idea of Equality* ❧
LEE HALL

My brother once asked my mother where babies came from. My mother was brought up in convent schools, had an arranged marriage, and used terms like "powder room." She was, however, prepared to give my brother an explanation, accompanied by educational materials that she had kept just for this moment. She said she had got us from the zoo. My brother looked bewildered. He asked what part of the zoo and my mother said that we were originally monkeys. And then I was equally bewildered because my brother insisted that monkeys had tails! And that's when I learned never to argue with my mother. She had a *National Geographic* magazine, featuring pictures of a rare "tail-less monkey."

When I was growing up, my parents had a business in Mexico and I was once taken to a bullfight in which three bulls were killed. It affected me in a profound way. (Equally disturbing was the fact that the scene did not affect others similarly.) My parents tried to "snap me out of it" by telling me the meat of the dead bulls fed the poor. In retrospect, I don't know why I didn't stop eating meat there and then. I think there was some vague sense of having no choice. Generally, the Great They said that humans had to eat meat or we'd die. Specifically, the issue of where the bull meat went seemed irrelevant; it failed to address my feelings about the bulls before they were meat. The suffering I witnessed could only be described as deliberate, slow torture.

My parents went on frequent business trips. I spent time traveling with my parents, and other times away at school. When I was at home, I lived with two beautiful dogs, Rom and Monty. Rom was eventually stolen and Monty was killed by a kennel keeper in a botched attempt to force him to breed. Monty's death hurt me in the way any loss of a human friend or relative would.

My mother trained, showed, and raced horses throughout her life. She taught me these things. I thoroughly enjoyed being with horses. I saw enough human insensitivity along the way, however, to cause me to avoid these activities as an adult. But the sight of wild horses still delights me.

When I began my university studies, I led a group that campaigned for the Equal Rights Amendment. The idea of equality dawned on me as something real and personal and essential. I began to understand that equality was not an academic theory; it was not sameness; it was not the relinquishing of individuality. It was not being "like" someone else or getting as much as others had. It was pure respect, and, as such, it couldn't be mathematically measured out and compared.

In 1983, I was living in England and attended a concert in Brixton, South London. Someone had placed leaflets on every fold-up chair. I read one of the leaflets carefully. It explained the effect of the holiday season on nonhuman animals. How many puppies were bought for children and later discarded, the number of furs sold, the number of geese and turkeys who ended up on platters, etc. I decided I should find the person who placed the flyers on the seats. Something about going to a concert with such a serious purpose was impressive.

That person was Robin and I met him and talked in the hall outside the concert arena. Robin had recently finished a prison term for a break-in at a chicken factory. He was not at the break-in, he told me, but he knew the people who were. As they had jobs and families, and he did not, he told the police he had done the break-in. In jail, the guards had taunted him for being a vegan. They had placed bets on when he would eat a ham sandwich, and they had given him no other food. This game had continued until he had suffered serious health consequences.

I could not imagine being as kind as this person was—it wasn't a matter of animals, it wasn't a matter of humans. Robin was completely kind in a way that bypassed categories and transcended measured amounts of what he could "afford."

I told him I would become a vegetarian. He invited me to see "The Animals Film," a really stunning project in which Peter Singer makes an appearance. I believe at that time it had been shown once on the BBC and then banned. A newer documentary, by Jennifer Abbot, called "A Cow at my Table," uses some of its footage, but without the detailed indictment of several government agencies, pharmaceutical giants, and the enormous vested interest of both groups in biomedical research and in the livestock industry. I stopped eating animal products and was sick for three weeks, running to the toilet, it seemed, every few minutes. So, I ate fish and cheese for one more year, and in 1984 I successfully left animal products to the animals. I read *Animal Liberation* by Peter Singer and the nexus of racism, sexism, and speciesism became clear.

In late 1996, I entered law school and spent most of my time connecting everything I was taught, for better or worse, to the history of slavery. I see no boundary line between the enslavement of humans and enslavement of other animals. I see slavery as very much alive; the line separating owner from property has merely inched over a bit. Our legal literature admits to only a limited number of mistakes at once.

I have been an invited speaker at the Washington Ethical Society. The subject of my talk was our moral obligations to nonhuman animals, and the philosophy of the Great Ape Project as a bridge to recognition of those obligations. I have also spoken about vegetarianism at a convention of the Florida Greens. More recently, I spoke at the Jane Goodall Institute's 1999 North American Youth Summit.

I am now immersed in research concerning the ownership of nonhuman great apes in human society. I am an associate at an immigration law firm and often notice similarities between the treatment of non-citizens and the treatment of nonhumans—more so than one might guess. When one visits a client who is being physically abused in jail it becomes clear—especially because clients charged with "deportability" are subject to incarceration not on the basis of any crime, but on the basis of their non-citizen status.

❧ *Teenage Vegetarian* ❧
HELEN

It's not easy being vegetarian, not easy at all, given that the majority of the population in the United States is omnivorous and is constantly keeping up the demand for meat. So why do people eat meat? Most families raise their children eating both plants and animals, not thinking twice about what it is they are really eating, and the pain involved in the process to make this "food."

When I was about nine I started to truly realize what I was eating. I had known before that I was eating pig or cow, but it didn't fully register in my head. I decided to eat meat anyway since it was always there and it tasted good. When I was twelve, the cruelty of eating an innocent, unwilling animal slapped me right in the face, when I saw a cow being killed on television. That summer, I went vegetarian, but I wasn't eating right and I got sick. My parents made me start eating meat for a few months, against my will. Sneaking most of the meat I was given to my dog, I remained somewhat vegetarian, eating meat about once a week. For my New Year's resolution in January 1998, being twelve (almost thirteen), I went vegetarian, and have been ever since.

A few months ago, I went vegan, but again I got very sick. I didn't adjust too well to the dairy alternatives, so I was only eating fruits, veggies, pasta (without eggs), and peanut butter sandwiches. So, for now I am sticking to a strict vegetarian lifestyle, and will go vegan later on when my dad won't kick me out of the house for doing so.

I do get a lot of negative criticism for being vegetarian. I usually hear that humans are at the top of the food chain and that we can eat whatever we please, or that the animals are killed mercifully so it's okay. These are the exact same ways I used to feel when I was younger, but now I realize they are ignorant and selfish feelings. Other people have had the nerve to wave a hamburger or leather shoe in my face, trying to upset me. I think the best way to deal with it is to tell them the truth—tell them how, contrary to their beliefs in humane slaughter, animals are killed unmercifully. If someone keeps criticizing after that, I usually just ignore them, because if they have no respect for my beliefs, then I'm not going to listen to them.

It's not too hard to find vegetarian food in restaurants, but vegan food is pretty hard to find. I advise going to the Pretzel Maker for a good vegan snack, since the store uses vegetable oil, not butter. Most restaurants that carry pasta have vegan food too.

I feel that the key to being vegetarian or vegan is to respect everyone as long as they aren't jerks about your choices, and to use education to teach people why they should be vegetarian.

First though, we need to fight against fur, animal abuse in homes, animal testing, and bestiality. Once we get most of that out of the way, more people will be willing to be vegetarian, because they will be more informed on the topic.

❧ *My Planet* ❧
INGRID NEWKIRK

Sometimes an odd experience or an unexpected relationship changes a person's life. A pig changed mine. So did a long-dead Indian poet named Rabindranath Tagore.

The pig and I met when I was an investigator for the humane society. I had driven thirty miles into the Maryland countryside on a blustery day to see if the man on the phone had told the truth: he had gone to a farm to read the gas meter, he said, and had found animal bodies strewn about like matchsticks.

The farmhouse was eerie and deserted, its doors flung open by the wind, its rooms littered with newspapers, unopened bills, trash. Whoever had lived there had left in a hurry. There was no sign of life in the fields either. However, once inside the rickety old barn, as my eyes adjusted to the darkness, I could see what the caller had been talking about. There were several horses, a brown dog on a chain, and a pile of pigs. They had all starved to death. All, that is, but one.

As I focused in on the faint moans coming from the darkest corner of the building, I could make out a tiny, pinkish-gray face. Like the other animals, this little pig had cut herself to ribbons on the broken glass that covered the barn floor. Yet, somehow, she was clinging to her life. She was too weak to stand, but so small and light that I carried her easily outside onto the grass. I could feel her body shivering in my arms, perhaps from the fever of her infected cuts. I laid her down, gently, under a tree. She hadn't even the strength to lift her head, so I held up her chin to let her drink water from my thermos cup. She chewed, as if in slow motion, the grass I offered her, falling asleep almost immediately after the third mouthful, her sweet little grunts of gratitude subsiding. It was impossible not to feel her pain.

That night, with her safely at the veterinarian's and my evidence gathered up, I drove home. "What can I fix for dinner?" I wondered, mentally inventorying the freezer. "Ah, I know. Pork chops."

It hit me like a thunderbolt. My job was to prepare legal charges against the people who had left the little pig to suffer. Yet here I was, about to eat a part of a pig for my dinner. Did I imagine that the pig whose bits were now in my freezer had enjoyed his or her experience on the factory farm and the killing floor any more or cried out any less than the little pig I had just held and comforted? "No matter how far removed the slaughterhouse," said the playwright George Bernard Shaw, "there is complicity." I was paying others to be cruel to animals while I ate the spoils. Did the fleeting taste of flesh matter more to me than their suffering?

That night I stopped eating animals. Later, I learned that, just as there are vegetarian alternatives to every food I ever fancied as a flesh-eater (including faux hot dogs, veggie burgers, and soy milks), there are compassionate choices to be made when it comes to clothing (fabric and cotton instead of leather and fur, for example) and to shampoos and cosmetics (no need to buy products tested by being poured down animals' throats when over 400 companies use modern non-animal tests, like computer assays).

As for Rabindranath Tagore, the poet and sage, years before my visit to that farm I had heard one of his disciples say that the most valuable lesson in life is to learn what is important and what is not. In the first category, Tagore put Earth and all the beings who live on her. His words had sounded ridiculously simple then, but the little pig who had slept in my arms under the tree had brought them to life.

We touch so many lives—some human, some not. My touch, sometimes made unthinkingly—say, when I bought cruelly tested hairspray or a ticket to the circus—had brought pain to others. After I started thinking about what I was eating, so much became clear.

Alice Walker, author of *The Color Purple*, summed up our casual tyranny when she wrote, "The animals of the world exist for their own reasons. They were not made for humans any more than black people were made for whites or women for men."

People talk a lot about peace, but Tagore and Walker pointed out to me that even in everyday things we can make peace happen.

❧ *Frat House Vegetarian* ❧
DR. JASON K. REDI

During the summer of 1989, I was living in my fraternity house with a few other brothers who were also staying around the university for the summer. One particularly hot afternoon, two of us went to eat at the local cheese-steak house. Cheese-steak houses are particular popular around the Philadelphia area and serve food which is about as grease-laden and gooey as carnivores will eat. So, there we were talking over blood, grease, and anonymous cheese mush on a very hot afternoon on a summer where we had probably been up till four in the morning drinking ourselves silly every night. We felt terrible and were not happy about it.

"Ever think about being vegetarian?" one of us asked the other.

"Yea, sure. Occasionally."

"Want to try it for a month?"

"OK."

And that was it. The two of us had to cook for ourselves for the summer anyway (no cook at the fraternity when there were only a few guys around). Both of us were fairly liberal and educated, so vegetarianism wasn't shocking. It was just something weird to try as a short experiment (like a new beer).

After a month of eating lacto-ovo-vegetarian food (though most meals wound up being vegan), we both felt healthier. We decided to keep going with it. (In retrospect we probably would have felt better just by not drinking and exercising a little bit—

but eating vegetarian was more fun than either of those alternatives.)

During this time, I was reading an issue of *Penthouse* (yes, there are very good articles in there). There was an article called "Green Rage" which was written by someone from People for the Ethical Treatment of Animals (PETA). It was all about the environmental and ethical implications of eating meat. I hadn't ever thought about it before, and had never read anything quite like this article. I think my mind was open to really thinking about it all because, at the time, I wasn't eating meat and could imagine never eating meat again.

I wanted more information, so I called *Penthouse* and tried to get the address of the author or PETA. (Remember, this was in the days before the Internet). Due to their privacy policy, the magazine could only forward mail that I sent to it and not give out addresses directly. I wrote, but never heard back. About a year later, I found the real address of PETA (I think in an issue of *Spin* magazine), and joined so I could learn more about the ethical and environmental side of vegetarianism.

I've been vegetarian for eleven years now and vegan for over a year. My friend who was at the steak house is still a vegetarian as well. We saw each other at a wedding a few months ago and agreed that neither of us have ever thought about going back.

❧ A Growing Awareness ❧

JEAN LAUREN

My vegetarian lifestyle evolved from a growing awareness of, and concern for, animal abuse. It gained momentum when my younger daughter refused to dissect an animal in a high school course. I supported her position and then she logically deduced that, if we opposed this cruelty, we shouldn't eat animals. At that time, I still believed the propaganda circulated by government, university, and vested interests that animal protein was a necessary part of our diet, but I agreed that we wouldn't eat young animals. Veal and lamb were no longer part of our diet.

Fortunately, I am a reader and in pursuing the issues of health, animal exploitation, and abuse, I realized that personally no more rationalization or compromise was possible and so for the past thirty years I have been an animal rights activist and vegan. I am sorry to report that no other family members or any friends choose to follow.

Being a vegan has affected my social life in that I prefer not to attend traditional Thanksgiving dinners and similar meat-eating events. If restaurants at least offer a vegetable-based salad on the menu, I will eat out.

When I first became a vegetarian and a vegan I directed a lot of criticism at meat-eaters, but I have since moderated my comments. Meat-eaters apparently are too intimidated by my position to argue, but the question, "what do you eat?" is frequently asked. Patiently, I repeat all the options, and it becomes apparent that no further discussion is necessary!

❧ Straight-Edge Vegan ❧
BRIAN EVANS

I was raised in a home with traditional American meals. Even when I was young, I did not like inflicting pain on animals. My grandfather and uncle took me on my one and only fishing trip when I was in elementary school. I remember hoping I would not catch any fish since I really did not want to harm them. Fortunately, we did not catch a single fish and I was relieved. I still did not make the full connection about the harm I was inflicting on animals by eating them.

In 1992, when I was sixteen years old, I became a vegetarian. This was after a great deal of thought and philosophical discussion with my two cousins and brother. We all decided to become vegetarians for the simple reason that animals feel pain. It was this philosophical premise of preventing suffering in others regardless of species that led me to stop killing animals.

I educated myself on all aspects of the animal abusing industries. Peter Singer's book, *Animal Liberation*, had a tremendous impact on me, since I came to vegetarianism through philosophical thought. In 1993, I became fully vegan. I realized that a vegan lifestyle was ideal since I did not want animals to be treated as slaves for humans. I learned of the abuses of the dairy industry and the connection with the meat industry. By 1994, I had become involved in activism for animal liberation and other political issues.

Around the time I became vegetarian, I became interested in a music scene called "straight-edge." A person who was straight-edge did not consume alcohol, drugs, or cigarettes and did not participate in promiscuous sex. Many straight-edge people were vegetarians and vegans. This really appealed to me. It is a lifestyle of self-improvement. I became straight-edge as well as vegetarian and later vegan.

When I initially became a vegetarian, my parents were very opposed to the whole concept. They even protested further when I became a vegan. It has been seven years since I became a vegetarian and six years since I became a vegan. Over that time, my parents have come to accept my lifestyle and show me some support.

I cannot imagine not being a vegan. I am healthier and I feel better about myself since I am contributing to the reduction of the suffering of others. When I was eighteen, I even had "vegan" tattooed on my left leg in gothic lettering. I knew I would never quit being a vegan. I urge others to think about the suffering inflicted upon animals and I hope they reach the conclusion that they should adopt a vegan lifestyle.

❧ *Unspeakable Suffering* ❧
DIANA COX

For many years I never thought about becoming vegetarian as, like most people, I failed to confront where my meat was coming from. The turning point came when I was confronted head on with the source of much of my diet.

I live in Hong Kong, and it's very easy to cross what used to be the border into China where, inevitably, one spends time tracking down cheap, local restaurants. I was with a group of friends, one of whom was Chinese-speaking and able to ask for the best deal in town. We ended up in a waterfront restaurant that was full of local people eating, drinking, and smoking with gusto. There were the usual ducks and chickens hanging in the window dripping grease as well as tanks of fish, crabs, scallops, and anything else that moved and lived in the sea. I had always found this food easy to resist as I suspected that the hygiene left much to be desired. However, on this occasion, I saw for the first time a "range" of food that I had never seen before. Among the fish tanks and the dripping carcasses were small, wooden cages of live rabbits and cats—some old, some very young, waiting to be pointed out by some customer, taken to the back, and killed to be eaten. There were price tags on the cages—cheap, very cheap. Cheap enough to allow one to rescue the entire contents of the restaurant. Were it not for the prohibitive quarantine restrictions in Hong Kong, we would have been tempted to have done just that. But we knew that, even if we had been able to rescue them all, there would be a steady supply of others to take their place.

Relating this story to friends in Hong Kong I realized my hypocrisy. Why was I so upset at the thought of eating cats and dogs when I happily ate bacon, beef, lamb etc.?

The rest is history.

Being vegetarian in Hong Kong is easy. Beancurd forms a staple part of the Chinese diet and soy milk is plentiful and relatively cheap. This is OK as long as you cook for yourself, but eating out can be a problem. There are, however, some excellent Indian and a number of Chinese vegetarian restaurants. European restaurants are more difficult to come by. The heat, humidity, and lack of refrigeration in markets means that many animals are killed at the point of sale. This is extremely disturbing to witness.

I find it incredible how people feel the need to challenge me over my diet. Being vegan, as I now am, I find I am called upon to justify my position as if it ran counter to every common sense principle in existence. Some people are aggressive, some quizzical, some patronizing. Few are respectful or accommodating. Friends have accused me of forcing my dietary preferences on them when they come to my house, objecting to the fact that, if I go to them, they have to eschew their normal diet to accommodate me, yet I don't reciprocate by providing them with their meat-based preferences. I try to explain the ethical arguments but, alas, they fall on deaf ears.

I now try to avoid defensive positions and ask people to tell me why they eat meat. Their replies come down to one thing: "I like the taste and I will not be morally blackmailed into giving up what I like, however much suffering you say I condone because, at the end of the day, I don't think animals suffer because, at the end of the day, they are only animals." Of course, people phrase what they say differently. They may even come up with subtler arguments. But, ultimately, it comes down to the same thing.

Like most vegetarians and vegans, I can think of many, disparate arguments against meat-eating: ecological, economic, health-governed, and philosophical. To me, these pale into insignificance set alongside the unspeakable suffering and cruelty of the meat industry. I don't think it will end in my life-time, but I do believe that the seeds have been planted so that, one day, people will look back on the "dark days" of meat-eating as we now look back on slavery or trial by ordeal: with profound sorrow and regret.

Out of the Cheese Trap

MARYANNE APPEL

I embraced vegetarianism (I am now vegan) almost twenty-seven years ago. My practice of veganism extends to the staunch support, without apology, of the destruction of property, when necessary, to save living beings. The brave ALFers are my heroes.

I am owned by two shelter rescuees, a dog, Chico, and a rabbit, Honey Bunny Bear, both absolutely marvelous companions and both vegans, to the extent that that is possible (rabbit pellets contain animal fat, and Chico's toothpaste is chicken-flavored).

Also sharing our home is my husband, Steve, who is a meat-eater, and who, while he does partake of many of my vegan meals, at times prepares flesh foods (while I absent myself from the kitchen), as well as vegetarian foods for himself.

Only vegan food is served to our guests, and I do not attend any affairs where flesh is served. This does cause some consternation among friends and family members at times; however, the suffering of animals raised for food is ever-present in my mind and I cannot endure watching anyone consuming the products of such terrible agony.

When I was a child of eleven or twelve years of age, I wanted to forego eating meat, having witnessed truckloads of cows being transported to the slaughterhouse in Philadelphia; however, I did not have the support of my parents and was not allowed to follow my conscience. During the years that followed,

I had qualms many times about the eating of animals but, in discussions with friends and relatives, I was always told that these animals were farm animals and were raised for the purpose of producing food. Somehow it still didn't seem right to me, but I kept on eating them!

When my conscience reawakened (at thirty-six years of age!), I stopped eating lobsters and crabs, having compassion on animals that were boiled alive. I recalled (after so many years of my first awakening to vegetarianism) my father cooking crabs in a huge pot, pushing them back in the boiling water time after time as the poor animals tried desperately to climb out of the pot to escape their agony.

Shortly after my liberation from the consumption of lobsters and crabs, I discovered the true joys of vegetarianism and turned away from the eating of flesh foods altogether. How I enjoyed my meals immensely, being freed from the twinges of guilt that had pursued me through the years! But tempering that joy was the terrible realization that confronted me every day (as it still does) that so many billions of innocent beings suffer so horribly so that people can enjoy eating their flesh. The brutal existence that these so-called "farm" animals are forced to endure is really too much to bear, not only for them, but for those of us who suffer with them every minute of every day.

Through the ensuing years, I seesawed from vegetarianism to veganism and back again. It was so easy for me to get caught in the seductive cheese trap! The hypocrisy of it all still stuns me! After so many years of conflict, I know now that I can never be anything but vegan, and the lightness of spirit that this way of life gives me is exhilarating!

❧ *Remembering Elsie* ❧
DIANA ENGORON

When I was seven years old, I went to the 1964 World's Fair in New York. All of our family came for the week and stayed with us as we were only twenty minutes from the fairgrounds. I remember going to the Borden exhibit and being totally fascinated with Elsie the Cow—being a city kid, I'd rarely get a chance to see a live cow!

The next day (a Sunday) my mom made dinner for everyone and she placed a platter down in the middle of the table. I asked her what the "red stuff" was and she told me it was blood from the roast beef. My uncle, always the joker, said, "Remember Elsie? That's either her or one of her family members!" Well, I screamed and yelled and carried on as children do and quit eating red meat. My mother was beside herself, worried that I would die because I wasn't getting enough iron (that's what moms worried about back then).

When I became a teenager, the chicken and fish went. Now, in my forties, I am about to become totally vegan. I stopped wearing leather in my thirties and now am proudly on my way to being vegan. In the beginning, I ate a lot of salad and veggies, and potatoes, but choices are much better these days. Of course, I prefer to prepare my own. I think it's healthier and certainly more cost-effective. I try to explain the facts, but most people don't bother me about it. They know I'm a lifelong animal person and a strong, outspoken woman, so I can pretty much turn things around and make people question their food choices.

❧ *Enlightened by a Daughter* ❧
DORIS SCHACK

I didn't become a vegetarian until I was fifty years old. I lived on a farm growing up and we killed chickens and cows. I feel terrible about it now.

About seven years ago, just before Thanksgiving, my daughter became a vegetarian, deciding that very day she would not eat another animal, not even turkey which used to be her favorite meat. She showed me her animal rights magazines and told me how awfully the animals were treated before they were slaughtered. I gave up everything except tuna fish, until one day I saw a film on tuna fishing. They were sawing the head off a live tuna as he was flopping around and I never ate tuna again.

I am so thankful my daughter enlightened me about this abuse. I cannot imagine how I ever ate animal flesh. I cannot stand the thought of it now.

People wonder why I don't eat meat and they ask if it is for health reasons. I tell them it is because I love animals too much.

My daughter and I are both animal activists now and have rescued many cats, dogs, rabbits, and birds.

❧ *Why I live Cruelty-Free* ❧
DUNCAN MYERS

The first fifty years of my life were pretty normal, eating the SAD (Standard American Diet) menu, wearing leather and wool, etc. But for various reasons, my wife and I were cutting down on meat and happened to pick up a copy of the magazine *Vegetarian Times.* This opened our eyes to a whole big veggie world that we didn't know existed! I didn't even know what vegan was, but now I am one!

There was very little use of the "v" words in western Michigan. We had no restaurants or groups to visit for information or support. We found a few things in libraries (and have subsequently donated many vegetarian materials) and began joining several national groups, to "get up to speed." We started a vegetarian society to find a few others with whom to share information.

The going was always too slow. We'd get the membership up to twenty and then a few would move away. Most people in the Midwest aren't vocal about being different from the norm and are very conservative. But I do know people pick up some of the literature that we spread around and that they are cutting back on animal products.

Also it seems that letters to the editor of our local paper seem to favor our positions more and more. A couple of years ago, we had about a dozen letters battling the hunters' position. That's the big reason for us to keep up all the communication— the other side can't win because our side is the higher position.

The facts all support the vegan lifestyle, so we can't lose unless we sit by and do nothing.

Having said that, let me add that having one side against the other is not the best way to a better world. We all start out as kids loving animals, not wanting to hurt them. We have to be taught to be cruel, to torture and eat flesh, and wear their skins. We want to tap into the common love for all animals that we had. All the other stuff will follow: better health for us, the planet, and of course the rest of the animal kingdom.

I'm selfish. I love being vegan. I find it very liberating...it's flat-out joy! It is probably the feeling that I always looked for in religion or politics, but could never find. The other day, upon lifting up the dish drainer, I spotted a little dark blob in the bottom of the sink. It was a waterlogged moth, not moving. I took the time to check it out and it moved a little. Carefully, I got it moved onto some dirt in a potted plant so it could dry out. A while later it was gone. I had saved a bug. Nobody but myself knew it, but I felt a joy that simply couldn't be topped.

That's what being a vegan is to me. It's all about helping others and, in a nifty turn, it helps you more than anything else ever could.

Now, let me cover myself a bit and say that religion and politics aren't all bad. There are, of course, good and bad people in both, so I usually stay away from arguing vegan ethics within those confines. To me, the vegan position is above all these other human institutions. It does not ask for money, your vote, your loyalty, or your time. It simply asks you not to hurt animals.

Of course, we are not perfect. Animal by-products pop up everywhere. Just when we thought we found the perfect vegan soup, the company reintroduces it with chicken broth.

We're all at a different level. We try and do better and we try to coach others the most effective way we know. And we try to relax and enjoy this compassionate lifestyle called veganism. We do it right, and though we might not even be trying to lead, others will follow!

❧ *Because I Care* ❧

ERIN MOORE

I am a vegan because I care. I don't just care about myself in this selfish world. I care about Earth and all of its inhabitants, mostly nonhuman animals. I also care about the health of my body and the condition of modern-day society.

I chose to become vegan about one and a half years ago after reading "Why Vegan?", a pamphlet I found on campus at Ohio State University. I couldn't help crying when I read the stories of true occurrences at farms. I realized, even then, that of course these atrocities didn't occur everywhere. But, I felt, if they are happening anywhere, then I had to fight to stop it.

People often ask me why I don't just eat free-range eggs, drink milk without recombinant Bovine Growth Hormone, or eat meat that has met tilth-standards. "First and foremost," I answer, "because it makes people ask me about it, and when they ask, maybe they will hear some things they didn't know and maybe I can spread the word to just one more person who cares." And then I say that there aren't ample restrictions and checks on those "happy animal products" and that the thought of eating animal products anymore makes me squirm.

The best activism or way to make people aware and thoughtful on a subject is to live what you preach, or walk what you talk. No one will listen if you aren't showing them what you are telling them. So many people out there are aware of some of the things going on and believe they are bad and shouldn't happen. However, they do nothing about them in their own lives except complain. That is no way to solve a problem. Hypocrisy is so prevalent here in the United States that it has become accepted as a way of life.

I don't get much criticism from people about my diet. Some people think I'm a vegan merely to stay healthy and thin, which of course is quite a nice side effect of being vegan. But that's not the case. I like it when people ask about my veganism. As long as you are serious and knowledgeable about your lifestyle choice, I think people will respect your decision. Of course, some people tease, but there are so many issues to bring up against meat-eaters that teasing them back is not hard!

I have never had a problem eating out. Nowadays, pretty much every restaurant has at least one vegetarian dish, and if it has cheese or something else non-vegan, the chefs can usually leave that ingredient out in the preparation. Even traveling across the country, I haven't had much of a problem. I did travel through the South once, which I had been curious to see, as the Pacific Northwest has quite a vegetarian community and ample choices when dining out. There was no problem.

When people examine my decision, they say, "Wow. It must be hard to eat," or something similar. "It's not," I answer, "you just have to know what things generally contain and learn to read a lot of labels." I don't eat much processed food, so it really isn't a problem when eating mostly fresh food. And, whenever I travel or stay at someone's house, I make sure to bring some snacks and maybe a carton of soy milk if the visit is longer than one night. I've gotten used to carrying food with me pretty much wherever I go. Because I am vegan and eat a lot of fresh, nutritious food, when I get hungry, I really get hungry! I feel this is because I don't have a bunch of crap in my system that can still be broken down when the stomach is empty. My body uses basically everything I put in it, and when the supply gets low, I can really feel it.

Some people also ask where I get my protein, and I answer that vegetarians don't have to worry about protein very much if eating healthily, and that what had been said before about the lack of complete protein in the plant world was proven false. Spinach, tofu, and quinoa have complete proteins, as well as other things. And I make sure, of course, to take my vegetarian supplements and calcium and iron every day.

I work out probably more than anyone I know—five days a week, about two to three hours a day. So, I am an excellent example of an extremely active vegan. I have felt no difference in my energy level since becoming vegan and can build muscle quite well. I do notice that my skin doesn't heal quite as quickly or as well as it did before (I scar more easily), but that could be also attributed to not being quite as young as before.

I've heard people say, "I could give up meat, but I couldn't give up milk and cheese," or some variation thereof. "Don't you miss ice cream? Don't you miss _____?" I answer that I don't miss it. "Indeed," I add, "there is no point to missing it, because I will never have it again, and that would be torture." Life is not about getting everything you desire, no matter the consequences. It is not about only *us*. It is about the system that surrounds and envelops us all. We can't always have everything we want—and we should probably make sure we don't.

There are certain needs we all have. Proper nutrition, shelter, and clothing would top my list. Food has become another one of America's obsessions. It isn't about giving our body ample nutrition for our day's activities. It's about satisfying or pleasing our taste buds, at the expense of our health and obviously now at the expense of the health and happiness of nonhuman animals as well. I feel our contemporary attitude is solely about humans and our every want and desire. And I don't buy into it anymore.

I have to make a difference in this world. The torture of animals cannot go on any longer. Nonhuman animals have as much of a right to their health and happiness as human animals do. Nonhuman animals need to be given, at least, the ability to have their *telos* or goal, their built-in, individual drive for happiness. For example, chickens have a need to scratch dirt, peck at the ground, and roam free; cows need to chew their cud; cats need to sharpen their claws, roam freely, and play with or hunt moving things. We all have needs for our happiness different from any other animal. And we all have the right to have our *telos* satisfied. Modern-day factory farming denies nonhuman animals their *telos*. They have become merely products, no longer living things.

That is why I am a vegan. Through my example, I hope that people will learn, listen, and understand. And hopefully people will change, and that will bring about change in our society. These practices are unacceptable. I believe if many people knew what really went on at farms, at least some of the time, they would come to think of it as unacceptable as well. It all starts with the individual.

And that is who I am.

❧ *Vegan for Health* ❧
JEANNE PITTS

In March 1990, I went to the doctor for a physical examination because I was having stomach problems and, in conjunction with that, I had a cholesterol test done. My cholesterol was borderline too high and even though I didn't have an ulcer, it was close. My doctor recommended I cut out alcohol, eggs, and red meat. So I did. I'm one of those types of people that can quit "cold turkey" when I make up my mind that that's what I want to do.

Later that summer, I met someone who was a vegetarian and, through talking with him, I decided to cut out all meat and to quit wearing leather and using other things made with animal by-products. I wasn't fully vegan, but I began moving in that direction. And so it's been a progression ever since. I've cut out caffeinated beverages, foods made with processed sugar, and a lot of other processed foods. A year ago, I finally cut out dairy products completely so I am mostly vegan (I'm not sure anyone can be fully vegan although they can come extremely close). I still consider it a progressive journey and I have many more miles to travel and many things to learn, but I'm very happy with my chosen diet and ethical consideration toward the treatment of other life. My latest venture is to try to eat more whole, fresh foods instead of cooked.

People don't really criticize me when I tell them I'm a vegetarian. I mainly get dumb questions like, "Do you eat fish or chicken?" or "How do you get enough protein?", and that type of thing. My mother says she doesn't understand but she accepts my diet. People are more curious, I think, than anything else. Also, people tend to think that once you cut out all the meat and everything you've cut down on your choices of what you can eat. While this is true in a way, I never fully appreciated the variety of fruits and vegetables that are available until I became a vegetarian. I don't miss any of the things I've cut out of my diet or that I've cut out in the way of animal by-products in the things I wear and use daily.

I would suggest that if you have an inclination to travel this path, do it. You won't regret it.

❧ *Elmo* ❧
ANN MARIE JOINER

I was a meat-eater for more than twenty years. I grew up in a household with no pets, except for a budgie who died. I was always intrigued by cats and dogs, but was really scared of them, as my mother had been attacked by two Siamese cats. Since then, it was like the shroud of shame to have a cat or dog, or even to think about it.

Then, two years ago, I met the love of my life, Jason. He is as close as it comes to being a vegan, but he eats milk products and honey (eggs are excluded). His principle is not to hurt any other living thing, meaning he will eat honey because it doesn't harm the bees, but will not buy leather shoes or belts because a cow was murdered to produce them.

I was *so* impressed with the way he handled things—the criticism, the questions ("where do you get your protein?"), as well as the annoyed waitress giving that blank stare when asked "is this soup meat- or vegetable-based?" I am sure you can understand this if you have ever been in a similar situation. I had tried previously (alone) to become a vegetarian for health reasons, but peer pressure got me to cave in. Now that I have Jason, I can truly form a united front, including handling the peer pressure.

I slowly gave up red meat, then white. I still had not given up fish of all sorts—until I met Elmo, our gray and white tabby. He is the cutest, cuddliest cat I have ever seen. He was found in a dumpster in Prince Edward Island by my sister-in-law. She heard Elmo's meows of hunger and sickness, and took him home to join the multitude of other cats she has. Unfortunately, my sister-in-law's home is right next to the Trans-Canada Highway, and a lot of her pets have met their death. We were concerned that if we left Elmo there, his days would be numbered, so we drove him fourteen hours to be with us at home in Montreal.

Elmo was *so* small, he could fit into the palm of my hand. The vet said that he was so sickly that he might not even make the ride home, because he had starved for too long, had lice, mites, and a heart murmur. The vet suggested we leave him, so as to not get attached. What the vet didn't know was that I already was. When I saw that helpless face, and the *need* to cuddle and make a home, I knew I couldn't continue to kill animals, especially such cute and cuddly ones as Elmo.

This is the day I gave up meat forever. I am so glad I made that decision. A few months ago, we got Elmo a girlfriend, Shyla, a petite black cat, from the Animal Rescue Network, a non-profit, no-kill animal shelter in Montreal. There are many other pets waiting for a home, and I encourage you to visit your local shelter to adopt them.

❧ *Cinderella* ❧
ALEXIS PREISSER

It wasn't any one thing thing that made me a vegetarian and animal rights and environmental activist. I was an only child and always had a dog. My dogs were my brothers, babies, friends, and confidantes. I loved all animals and would save frogs, birds, hedgehogs, whomever I thought was in trouble, injured, or in danger. My mother would sometimes be abusive to my dogs and this would pain me. She also got rid of all my dogs, sooner or later, and this is something I have never forgiven her for.

I never liked meat, but I realized that the food on my plate was a living, breathing creature when I was five. I had been given a lamb as a pet. I named her Cinderella and she was my love. One day, when she was grown, I couldn't find her at all. I don't know what they told me, but when I was served my dinner I knew it was Cinderella. Of course, I didn't eat it and to this day I have never eaten anyone. My heart was broken and I hated my mother. To this day, we have a troubled relationship due to her uncaring ways, but she denies that that is the cause of the friction. I have three kids and six dogs and, no matter what, my dogs will always be with us because they are our family.

Ten years ago, I became a voice for animals and have endured criticism and jokes. I work in law enforcement and am the butt of agents who find all the rescues and my dedication to liberating animals from a life of pain and abuse incomprehensible—although this attitude has changed somewhat because I tell them about extreme cases of abuse. I also inform them about factory farming in excruciating detail so they realize the muck the animals are fed, muck that in turn goes into people's bodies. I show them photos of factory farming. Many women in my office have switched from the menopausal drug Premarin™, made from the urine of pregnant mares, to soybean-based alternatives. Some have switched their consumption of beef to chicken. I tell them of the benefits of eating a vegetarian-based diet. The fact that I'm forty-six and look much younger helps to convince them.

My children are vegetarians also, not because I forced them to but because they read everything regarding animals—the newsletters from People for the Ethical Treatment of Animals and FARM, *Animal Liberation* by Peter Singer, etc. My children decided to live a cruelty-free life and are very active regarding animal rights and volunteering at shelters.

We dine out rarely because most places have limited and boring vegetarian fare. I am an excellent cook and have a large collection of cookbooks. With all the soybean products on the market today, it is very easy to substitute meat with a soy product and have it tasting the same if not better. When we have gone to a restaurant we make a request that they have meat substitutes and/or vegetarian fare that is tasty and attractive. If the restaurant doesn't serve it we leave. Usually, the next time, the restaurant will have added something vegetarians can eat.

Being a vegetarian makes me feel cleaner, better, and healthier. The idea of eating an animal would be tantamount to cannibalism because I know animals have emotions. The labeling of an animal as stupid and fit to be eaten is a fallacy. The only stupid animal I have met has been human.

❧ *Awakening* ❧

LESA MILLER

I was raised on the typical American meat-and-potatoes diet as a child with meat at almost every meal in some form or another. My favorite was grilled steak, charred black on the outside and bloody rare inside! I didn't know any vegetarians then, so I never had reason to question my eating habits.

In graduate school, my roommate was vegetarian. I asked her why and she responded by saying she didn't like the way meat felt and tasted in her mouth. I had never expected that answer, but I accepted it. A few years later, and after being married for just over one month, all at once I stopped eating all meat except for seafood. This was the result of an "awakening" I experienced while attending an animal rights conference in Philadelphia, Pennsylvania with a friend.

I had been interested in animal rights, off and on, for a few years, but had never looked into it as deeply as I did that weekend. All it took was seeing the videos, reading the literature, and listening to the speakers to turn me into a blithering idiot. I remember being embarrassed because I cried through the vegetarian and vegan buffet on the last day and some of the talks because I was so overwhelmed with information. It seemed the only logical thing I could do was to embrace what I learned and apply it to my own life. I truly had a new philosophy of life, a new way of looking at creatures I had always loved, but now with new knowledge and appreciation. Ever since then, I've been involved in animal rights, whether protesting, leafletting, letter writing, giving membership donations, etc. And I gave up all seafood and dairy products long ago, too.

Nowadays, it's not enough that I'm the student. I want to teach others about the animal issues that are so painful to hear, yet so satisfying to educate others about. I used to feel a sense of urgency about it; but, now that I'm older, I choose to educate others with a more savvy approach.

Humane education is in its infancy, but I foresee schools using it on a regular basis in the future. It's amazing how the same information can be relayed by two different people, in two different ways. This can mean the difference between a highly effective program and a bomb! The facts are a constant, but presentation is (almost) everything to an audience.

It takes persistence and confidence to stand up to those who ridicule and lash out at animal activists. I try to keep in mind that they are people who haven't yet seen and felt the cruelties that I have witnessed. I used to be like them.

❧ *Vegetarianism and Me* ❧
ALISON WEBB

I became a vegetarian just over a year ago, when I was eighteen. Coming to this stage, I knew at some point in my life I would stop eating animals; the only question was when. I have always had compassion for animals, but I did not feel ready to make any changes to my diet, and did not want to understand how animals were involved in the food process, until I was old enough to cope with it.

My older sister was the only person I knew who was a vegetarian and, if she hadn't made me aware of the facts, I don't think I would have been encouraged or inclined to try a vegetarian lifestyle. It was unfortunate that our parents have always been meat-eaters, so we were brought up to accept that killing animals for food was quite natural, acceptable, and pretty much essential.

I gave up eating meat, poultry, and fish overnight, once I had decided that I wanted to be a vegetarian. The actual moment when I made my decision was when my sister showed me what could only be described as a horrific leaflet, which she had gotten from one of the groups to which she belonged, on the treatment of poultry ready for slaughter. Due to my squeamish nature, I find any literature or visual aids of animal cruelty very distressing and, once I was aware of the facts associated with this, I could not carry on eating meat or animal derivatives.

I find it very difficult to find exciting foods or any food that is suitable for vegetarians as I am not adventurous and tend to just want food to fall in my lap without actively searching for it.

Dining out can also be a problem, as all of my friends are meat-eaters with no desire to try vegetarianism. The cause of the problem is finding a suitable restaurant that caters to everyone. Very often, restaurants have only a few vegetarian options that are not as varied as the meat options.

I am fairly passive when I receive criticism or get told the "alternative" view, mainly because I have my view and I know others have theirs, but I do not have the facts and figures in my head or at my fingertips to spout off to them in defense. I do not get into arguments except with people close to me, since I tend to care more about their attitudes than just casual acquaintances. I wish that the people in my life, especially partners, were vegetarian, as I find it an area where there is always disagreement because of our differing attitudes. I feel there is no point in wasting energy arguing with those who do not care about the facts and would not be vegetarian in any event.

I do not understand how anyone can willingly eat the flesh of a living being who is as deserving of freedom with rights like any other living being. As living creatures, capable of feeling pain, neglect, loneliness, boredom, maternal instincts, and many other feelings, I feel that we need to protect all creatures from abuse. It may seem hypocritical, considering I've only been a vegetarian a short while, and therefore must have thought like everyone else at one time. I knew killing animals was wrong, but didn't challenge it until recently. I believe the slaughtering of animals and the cruelty involved is unnecessary, causing pain and suffering that we as humans have no right to inflict on another living being. We have no right to dominate animals and deny them their freedom.

Another relevant issue, though not my main reason for giving up meat, is that valuable land is wasted feeding animals reared for meat. I was first aware of this in my first year at university while taking a course on the developing world. I learned that meat-eaters indirectly support and inadvertently cause the starvation of people living in less economically developed countries. The reason for this is due to the exploitation of land in poorer countries by industrialized countries such as the United States, Britain, and Japan. The land is used to produce food for animals that will be exported. Therefore, the land cannot be used for growing crops for the population's own consumption. This leads to widespread famine and many unnecessary deaths. Grain crops are the staple diet of poor countries. So, while others starve, we are being supplied with more than we can consume and do not even need to have.

I feel that my future as a vegetarian is very secure as I am sure my feelings will never change concerning animal well-being. I am optimistic about the future decline of the meat industry and believe that, one by one, people will come to realize that eating meat is not the best option for them or for the animals. If I have children, I will bring them up as vegetarians and teach them respect for all living things.

❧ Stranger in a Strange Land ❧

DAVE SNOWDON

I'm a raw-food vegan and, although I'm English, I currently live and work in Grenoble, France. I've been here for over three years now and am having fun trying to be a 100 percent raw tee-totaling vegan in a land where consuming meat, cheese, and wine are national pastimes.

So how did I get here? Well, my first foray into vegetarianism was sometime around March or April 1990, I was twenty-one at the time and in the final year of my undergraduate studies at Manchester University. The first British beef crisis was in full swing and I decided that it was not a good idea to eat red meat at that time and so dropped that from my diet. The whole issue aroused my interest and I started trying to find out a little more about the meat industry and the effects of meat on health. I didn't like what I found. I decided that meat was of dubious health value and that there was much inherent cruelty in the way animals were raised and slaughtered for food in Britain. I then adopted a mostly vegetarian diet, although I still ate fish for another year or so. I finally decided to stop eating fish partly due to environmental grounds (I'd heard that over-fishing had drastically lowered fish stocks to a unsustainable level) and partly on health grounds after reading how fish were contaminated by the pollution the industrialized countries were regularly discharging into the seas.

Although other members of my family (including one of my cousins) had experimented with vegetarianism before me, I was the only member of my family to go vegetarian and stick at it for more than a couple of months. I did find it awkward at first, since it seemed as if I had to continually justify my diet to everyone I happened to eat with, whether they were friends or members of my family. Eventually, I got used to explaining that I was vegetarian on both health and moral grounds and that seemed to be enough. At the time, my knowledge of nutrition was very rudimentary and I was not eating a particularly healthy diet. Although I could make a basic curry, I was not a great cook and was relying far too heavily on cereals, veggie-burgers, and junk food and was not consuming anything approaching enough fresh fruit and vegetables. Ironically enough, even though I was vegetarian I did not care very much for eating vegetables. It took another four or five years before I finally got bored and fed up of this diet and taught myself to cook more than a basic curry and eventually found the courage to start inviting friends to dinner. In the meantime, I studied for a Ph.D. and then moved to Nottingham to work as a research assistant for Nottingham University.

In November 1996, when a new neighbor moved into the flat next to mine in Nottingham. We had a couple of interests in common and ended up talking a lot about various things including nutrition. At this time, I'd been vegetarian for about seven years, but still ate a lot of cheese, sweets, and potato chips and drunk a lot of beer, coffee, and tea. I still stood out as the only vegetarian in my family and some of my relatives seemed regularly surprised that I looked reasonably fit and healthy without any meat in my diet.

Ravi, my new neighbor, had rather strange ideas about nutrition (or so it seemed to me at the time) and didn't drink tea, coffee, or alcoholic drinks and was, therefore, obviously somewhat weird (again as I thought at the time). After a chat one evening, she lent me *Raw Energy* by Leslie and Susannah Kenton. I was initially very skeptical, but I read the book. Six months later, I had become a vegan, given up alcoholic drinks, tea and coffee, and junk food and was trying to maintain a diet with a high percentage of raw food. My weight dropped very noticeably and I felt good. I'd been concerned about giving up my traditional programmer's diet of coffee and junk food because I wondered how I'd maintain my alertness and concentration at work. In fact, substituting herbal teas for tea and coffee resulted in me being no less alert and considerably less hyper.

Ravi had also become a very good friend both in terms of the fact that we got on well together and the fact that the front doors of our apartments were no more that a foot apart. Six months later, when they finally found out, my family reacted to the news that I'd gone vegan quite entertainingly. My mother who'd been prepared to tolerate a vegetarian was sure that a vegan diet was far too extreme and could not support life. I think that only the fact that I'd already been following this diet for several months and yet looked and felt great managed to keep her concerns to manageable levels.

Again thanks to Ravi, I also started running again and began to think about what I wanted to do with my life. At the end of 1997, my company offered me a job working for their research center in France. I'd been to France a few times for holidays and had loved it and had wanted to progress beyond my schoolboy French for some time. So, after a weekend of soul-searching, I decided that I couldn't pass up this opportunity. I quit my job at Nottingham University and moved to France. I was scared shit-

less by the change from my previously too-comfortable existence, but I've learned a lot about myself in the process and now
know that it was absolutely the right thing to do.

In May 1998, I completed a half-marathon; which I feel
shows fairly convincingly that being vegan and mostly raw has
done my health no harm at all! In November that year, I read a
book by the organization Nature's First Law. This has an uncom-
promisingly 100 percent raw, 100 percent natural food stance
and convinced me to at least try moving to a 100 percent raw
diet. Since then I've managed to stay (as near as I can tell) 100
percent raw for up to three months at a time. While I have not
yet noticed a great change in my physical health, I now feel
more full of the joy of life and take more pleasure in eating fruit.
I remember clearly one evening coming home from work and
feeling an intense desire to eat fresh fruit. Never had a meal
tasted so good! Each fruit (apple, orange, pear, kiwi) tasted
divine! It was as if I'd rediscovered something that had been lost
a long time ago. Since then, eating fruit has been a pleasure and
not something to be done purely for health benefits.

Eating out with friends, either at restaurants or at someone's
house has occasionally proved to be a struggle—especially in
France. In the early days, I compromised my vegan stance and
occasionally ate some dishes containing either cheese, milk, or
eggs, since I thought that friends who were used to a meat-based
diet were already going out of their way by cooking me vegetarian food. Now I'm a little surer of my friends and myself I
tend to stay vegan if I possibly can. Most restaurants in France
will serve a salad and so I can get by on that.

Being a 100 percent raw-food vegan has been more prob-
lematic than being simply a vegan and, while I'm perfectly

happy to order a salad in a restaurant, I don't yet feel confident enough to follow the lead of other raw-foodists and ask for a salad or fruit when eating at a friend's house. I feel that friendship is more important than having the occasional cooked meal, and so I still tend to compromise on this issue. I feel strongly that I should not try and impose my lifestyle on others, but I haven't decided if my reluctance to insist on being 100 percent raw with others is due to this or simply me being a wimp and afraid of being thought stranger than people already think I am.

Naturally, being in France, my diet stands out as being unusual and has attracted a lot of attention when I eat with people who don't already know me. I've always tried to avoid having a missionary attitude. While I think that a vegan lifestyle is better in terms of health, environmental grounds, and the overall reduction of animal suffering, I think that the best way to change people's ideas is by example rather than telling them they are wrong. I simply try to follow a diet that works well for me and, if asked, I will explain that I avoid all meat and dairy products because I feel healthier and want to avoid the cruelty inherent in the meat industry. Depending on my listeners' desire to discuss and/or debate with me, I might then explain why I follow a raw diet and go into more detail about nutrition and how enzymes are destroyed by cooking.

❧ *A Sense of Compassion* ❧
Ilse Marie Baca

Discussing my reasons behind compassionate living is very difficult for me. It is so intertwined with my very breath that it becomes almost painful to untangle its essence and confine it with words. All in one moment, my sense of compassion becomes overwhelming. I think about the thousands of moments that culminated in the self I am today. All the pictures, puppies, cattle trucks, and feed stores. The rotten smells churning from fast food chains, the wise eyes of creatures with four furry legs. The lessons of patience, humor, and loyalty that I've been taught from "dumb animals." It is such a long road, if only more people would be brave enough to travel it, they'd soon learn it becomes a beautifully rewarding one.

My grandmother told me recently that I've always been sensitive when it comes to animals. Not only animals, it seems, but all creatures. She recalled a time, when I was about three years old, when after having watched "The Fly" with her, I apparently went around the house for a couple of days with my face scrunched, my hands up, and with a tiny voice saying, "help me, help me." We laughed when she told me that story. But then my grandmother recoiled gently in deep thought, and almost to herself, she muttered, "What a strange thing for a child to do."

Being sensitive has just been natural to me. Indeed, it appears to be strange to some. My only regret, is not realizing sooner the secrets behind food production. I know that if I had been aware, as a child, of the torture behind what was being fed to me when

I was munching on the all-American hamburger, enjoying spaghetti with meatballs, or just drinking milk, I would have cried for days. But, how was I supposed to know that I was eating an animal with a mother? An animal who lived its entire life quietly whispering, "help me, help me."

In my early teens, I made up my mind to become a vegetarian. Unfortunately, it took a few years for the transformation to finally take root and become an integral part of who I was. When the ideals finally married into my seventeen-year-old lifestyle, I found the transition wasn't going to be easy. My family didn't know why I stopped eating meat overnight. I think it must have just been confusing. The normal breakfast, lunch, or dinner became a breakdown of ingredients, a struggle with my defiant sense of right or wrong. Patterns are always hard to break, especially the bad ones.

I look back now on what makes someone decide to break from the norm, to defy the existence of torture for food, medicine, and development. I believe it is an innate sense of understanding, a need to be aware instead of contently cloistered. And no, I don't think some people are born sensitive, while others are born to burn rain forests and eat cooked flesh. It is an awareness that is learned and nurtured like any other.

It's hard to know I can't save them all. I just keep in mind the world I'd love to live in. A world, no matter how strange it may seem to others, where a "food chain" does not exist. Where creatures do not terrify, torture, and ingest other creatures for power, sustenance, or need.

Someday, there will be no more "meat," no more fear, and no more industry inspired patterns of heart attacks, cancer, and murder. Someday, I believe, we will all wake up from this dream, and begin living as the true guardians of our diverse planet.

❧ *An Epiphany* ❧
Susan S. Barber

Ihave always loved animals. When I was a child, I planned to become a veterinarian because I thought that was the best way I could help animals. Even as a teenager, in junior high and high school, when we were all trying to figure out what we were going to do with the rest of our lives, I knew I would do something to help animals. I thought about being a wildlife biologist. I thought about finding a career that didn't directly help animals, but that would pay me well enough that I could give a lot of money to animal organizations. It turned out there was a very direct and easy way I could help animals that didn't have anything to do with choosing a lifelong career—becoming a vegetarian.

It all came to a head when I was in my second year of college. I was writing a speech for a public speaking class about predator "control." At that time, I was very much enchanted by the beauty and magnificence of wolves, so I decided to give a speech about our government's programs to eradicate the wolf. Amazingly, I didn't realize until doing research for this speech that the main reason predators are eliminated is because of ranching interests.

Cattle ranchers want to be able to run their cows freely (usually on public lands, I might add) without any threat of predators killing any of their "merchandise." So, the U. S. government has kow-towed to their demands for predator elimination. I realized then that if the public didn't buy from cattle ranchers, then ranchers wouldn't have the monetary power to control the lives of predators like wolves. I decided that if I cared about wolves, I would have to stop eating cows. Of course, I didn't think about the plight of the cows at that time. But that realization was a tiny seed that would soon sprout.

Around the same time I had that speech class, I met a woman named Jessica who was a vegetarian. I remember being intrigued by her, because she was different from most of the people in my classes. Still, I didn't think of becoming a vegetarian myself until I came home from class one day and my mother had cooked a ham. It was sitting on the kitchen counter, and there was a large bone protruding from it. My mother offered me some and I just looked at that bone and suddenly felt sick. Everything had come together: the realization that what I eat affects the world, the knowledge that there were people out there who did not in fact eat animals, and the sudden understanding that a piece of meat was in fact a piece of a dead animal. Very soon after all of this came together, I became a vegetarian and then a vegan.

I was sitting in my house one day, just thinking about it, and I knew I wanted to stop eating meat. But I went further (I've always been an all-or-nothing kind of person). I realized that if I loved animals, as I had felt all my life, then I should stop eating all animals and stop participating in their exploitation. If I was going to stop eating cows, shouldn't I stop eating cheese, too? Producing dairy products surely required the exploitation of cows. Shouldn't I stop eating eggs? After all, they were potential chickens. And if I was going to stop eating animals, shouldn't I stop wearing them? In a matter of minutes, I had decided to stop eating meat, dairy, eggs, and to stop wearing leather. I even decided that, somehow, I would not feed my dog dead, tortured animals, either. (It turns out there are quite a few vegetarian dog foods on the market and, today, my eight-year-old dog is thriving as a veggie dog, and still acts like a puppy!)

Soon after that, I found John Robbins' book, *Diet for a New America*. I read it with excitement, feeling as though it validated my choices. It also opened my eyes to the gritty details of animal agriculture and I knew that I would never go back to eating animals again. My family and friends were, of course, very surprised and concerned. A lot of people told me I would not be able to live a healthy life if I didn't eat at least some meat, or if I didn't drink at least some milk, but I ignored them all. I knew I had made the right decision. In fact, I think I may have been born to be vegan. When I was a baby, my mother tells me, I disliked meat and eggs and I would not drink cow's milk. I would take my bottles of milk and put them into the toilet! I knew intuitively what was not right for me.

Almost five years later, my life is so different from before I was vegan that I cannot even remember it. I can't believe I used to eat at McDonald's™ and Taco Bell™ almost daily! Becoming a vegan opened my eyes to so many things I had never thought of before, like the environment, world hunger, and human rights. I have become an activist and I relish the role. I enjoy knowing that, every day, just by picking up a fork, I am changing the world.

❧ *Vegetarian Sissies?* ❧

Erik Marcus

Some people like to label vegetarians as sissies or freaks. I'll concede the point that it's possible to find strange vegetarians, just as it is easy to find strange people who follow any other diet. But what some hold as sissified is really the starting point of a new way of looking at the world. At the core of vegetarian philosophy is a concern for personal health, for the environment, for world hunger, and for animals. And it hinges on what the late animal rights activist Henry Spira called the "nonviolent dinner table."

The *Economist* editorializes: "To see an animal in pain is enough, for most, to engage sympathy. When that happens, it is not a mistake: it is mankind's instinct for moral reasoning in action, an instinct that should be nurtured rather than mocked."

History's list of famous vegetarians reads like a roll call of the greatest thinkers and gentlest souls civilization has yet produced: Leonardo Da Vinci, George Bernard Shaw, Isaac Bashevis Singer, Mahatma Gandhi, Leo Tolstoy, and dozens more. Society's best and brightest have been attracted to this diet for 2,000 years, even when society at large dismissed vegetarianism as dangerous or odd.

Today it's not just eminent people who follow a vegetarian diet. People of all ages and all walks of life are becoming vegetarian and vegan. Perhaps it's because people are better informed about health than ever before. Or perhaps we are gradually learning to value compassion.

The typical American diet puts us at war with animals, the environment, even our own bodies. Whatever one's reason for becoming vegan, it is at bottom an act of compassion, and compassion can become an act of deep transformation. If you are what you eat, switching your diet remarkably changes who you are. After becoming vegan, many people find their health improving over the months and years. Perhaps this improved health sets the stage for a spiritual awakening that often follows. This awakening may take years, but ultimately you are likely to find yourself a different being than the one you were before you changed your diet. This awakening is, I believe, open to anyone.

There are few choices as vital as what to eat, and yet many people still don't make the connection between what they eat and what they believe. A person can become a teacher or social worker in order to make the world a better place, without considering that dining on animals three times a day is doing just the opposite. Other people plan fitness programs without first making the decision to keep their systems free from dietary cholesterol, saturated fat, and animal protein.

It was once mainly the greatest thinkers in history who weighed the consequences of their diet. Today, almost everyone has the resources to reconsider their food choices. It is an awakening whose time has come.

✎ *An Innocuous Picture* ✎
VEDA STRAM

The photo looked completely innocuous until I looked more closely at the picture and then read the header. There was a rope tied around the kitten's neck, attached to a long pole lying on the ground.

The caption read: "Boiled cat meat is considered a delicacy in many parts of the world."

I am one of those fortunate people in the world who was lucky enough to look at that photograph and get it immediately. Having lived with cats and kittens all my life, having my room-mates always include cats and kittens, having my best friends be cats and kittens, I immediately realized that every cow and every pig was as unique and special as each and every cat or kitten I had ever known.

I was instantly vegetarian.

Six months later, not having eaten a morsel of flesh, a wild pigeon (later named Peaches by me in honor of an infamous cat experimented on at University California, Los Angeles) appeared in my life, wounded, almost dying. She recovered under my care very nicely, sleeping in a cage at nights and walking or jumping or flying wherever she wanted all day.

I woke up one morning and removed the bright blue blanket from her cage where she had spent the night. She stretched her right foot back as far as she could and yawned, and then she stretched her right wing as high as she could and yawned again. And then she stretched her left leg as far as she could and yawned, and then she stretched her left wing as high up as she could and yawned.

And again, immediately, I was fortunate enough to realize, "Oh my god, battery hens...."

That had me be vegan instantly. I didn't even need to think about dairy after that. I was sure that the realities of dairy cows and their children would be just as earth-shatteringly awakening to me as the kitten by the "hot tub" and Peaches' stretching had been.

We cannot really "be vegan" in this world of animal pieces in car tires or elsewhere, but we can read labels and we can ask questions and we can always say very graciously, "No, thank you, but I don't eat animals" to anyone, under any circumstances, anywhere.

I am not a strict vegan. There is nothing strict or rigid about what I eat or drink or use. I am a committed, compassionate human being always thinking about the opportunity I have to be an example for others.

❧ The Power of a Magazine Article ❧
ALICE SAVAGE

I became aware of animal abuse and animals being slaughtered for food by reading an article in a magazine. It is no exaggeration to say that this article completely changed my life.

I had never really thought about where food comes from. In this I believe I was no different from many others, who don't think about where they get their hamburgers, steaks, bacon, etc. from. After reading the article, I started examining how I lived my life and decided to become a vegetarian and never eat meat again. I joined animal rights groups and enjoyed working to help the animals. I read a lot and learned quite a bit about the animal rights movement, and found myself in agreement that people do not have the right to exploit and kill animals for food to satisfy their stomachs. Simply put, I believe that animals were not put here on earth to provide us with food and entertainment. I believe that animals feel pain the same way we do and deserve to be respected.

I do get criticism from people, but find that the best way to handle it is to explain why I don't choose to eat meat and educate people on the cruelty of factory farming and slaughterhouses. I feel the only way to change the abuse of animals is through education. A lot of people I have talked to said they never thought about where their food comes from. Also, I know that a lot of people are interested in what it is like to be a vegetarian. Some people also don't know that you can live a completely healthy life without eating meat. Again, the key is education and giving people informed answers, so they can hopefully remember what you said the next time they eat a meal.

Through my example, I have caused my own family to cut back on their meat consumption and to make changes in their life. I have not personally found it as big a problem eating out as it once was, because so many restaurants offer vegetarian alternatives. I have discovered that, if you cannot find something on the menu, the chef will usually make something special for you if you request it.

❧ Mr. Monday ❧

JANE VELEZ-MITCHELL

To me vegetarianism is a consciousness, a state of awareness. Hence, it is a mark of evolution forward. My mother achieved that heightened consciousness as a child. She was living in Vieques, an island off the coast of Puerto Rico, and she had a pet pig. One day, she was returning home from school when her nostrils detected the unmistakable smell of roasted pig. She became hysterical. Then, when her family tried to offer her slaughtered companion to her as dinner, she became filled with rage. She refused to eat and became a vegetarian. That was the spirit with which I was raised. Still, my own life contained an early experience of animal cruelty. I had a dog, Mr. Monday, who was my love. He was not well-trained, but I was too young to understand that. One day, I came home from school and Mr. Monday was gone. To a farm, they told me. I did not believe them. I was heartbroken. I still cry the second I think about Mr. Monday. Everything I do for animals has within it the spirit of Mr. Monday and my sadness over his disappearance.

I have been a television news anchor and reporter for almost a quarter of a century, working most recently in Los Angeles and previously in New York City, Philadelphia, Minneapolis, and Fort Myers, Florida. All that time, I have been vegetarian and—for the last five years—vegan. Not only has that choice not interfered with my work, it has given me the energy to vigorously pursue my career. I also have enough energy left to run my website VegTv.com, which is a streaming video site that runs videos on vegetarian cooking and the vegan lifestyle. I use the technology of the new millennium to help Americans switch to a diet for the new millennium.

Since going vegan, I have felt much healthier. I've stopped experiencing the flu and cold symptoms that had previously plagued me through most of the winter months. Allergy to dairy is one of the most common, undiagnosed symptoms in America today. If you are suffering from dandruff problems, acne, frequent sinus infections, or colds, give up all dairy products for a month or two and switch to a diet high in unfried vegetables and fruits. See the difference for yourself!

My vegetarian mother used to get teased by her contemporaries, who mocked her for throwing parties where she served trays of vegetables. Today, she is in her mid-eighties and works out daily, dancing and lifting weights. All of the people who made fun of her are, sadly, no longer alive. We are living examples of the power of a pure, clean, and simple vegetarian diet, rich in nature's bounty of fruits and nuts, vegetables, and grains. Needless to say, exercise and the avoidance of other harmful substances, like alcohol and cigarettes, are prerequisites to benefiting from a vegetarian lifestyle. Alcohol and cigarettes are two substances that I have given up in the course of my sometimes arduous journey toward good health.

Open the book of history and you will see on the first page that mankind's partnership with animals as one of the earliest marks of civilization. But, if you open the last page, the most recent page, you will still not see the development that will, one day, truly signal mankind's genuine civilization, namely, his ability—no, his willingness—to survive without killing another creature. We already have the ability to survive without the taint of any meat or skin. We simply lack the consciousness—collectively. as a society—to know that such consumption is unnecessary and harmful, both to us and to the animal.

We understand, intellectually, from medical research, that the heavy consumption of foods laden in animal fats are bad for us, increasing our chances of developing heart disease, cancer, and a host of other illnesses. This is not fringe or radical. Organizations as mainstream as the American Cancer Society are publicly recognizing the value of eating a diet rich in fruits and vegetables. We see the development of plagues, such as mad cow disease, creating a panic. Still, we don't change.

Luckily, now, for the first time in history, we have alternatives! There are a growing number of meat substitutes going on the market that are delicious, low in calories, fat, and cholesterol and meat-free. With names like "Neat Loaf" and "Phoney Baloney" these products look and taste like meat and chicken, but they are made out of soy. You can find them at most health food stores and the mainstream supermarkets. And if you can't find them, tell the store manager you want them!

For me, it's simply a question of being guilt-free. I wake up, have a breakfast of fruit and grains, go to work and have a lunch of salad, come home, have a dinner of tofu and vegetables. All the while I know I have not hurt any other creatures to stay alive.

That, to me, is feeling evolved. A banana, a salad, tofu, grains, they are all delicious and fill me with a satisfaction where nothing got hurt and I did not hurt myself. The food I eat keeps me on the path to higher consciousness and self-awareness. Some people I know will never get there. Others I can see on the road. Life is a journey and what you eat to fuel you on that journey will determine how far you can travel and where you want to go.

❧ *Listen Carefully Before It's Too Late* ❧
INGRID NEWKIRK

My father died recently. Are all such deaths followed by feelings of missed opportunities, words that might have been spoken? I had no idea he knew he was dying and that this was the last time we would talk in person. All I knew was that I had a plane to catch, back to Virginia. It didn't occur to me then that, despite worsening pain, he treasured each moment that night, asking me to stay and talk to him at the dining room table as my mother cleared away the dinner dishes. He was too weak to sustain the conversation well and I found the going tough.

We have always been polar opposites on politics, and much else. He was a fearless adventurer, never happier than when out on his boat during a fierce storm, while I get seasick on a calm day. I was a disappointing "son," a girl who didn't appreciate his explanations of the Marconi wireless and a woman who can only turn on a television, not build one, as he did, from scratch. He wanted Al Haig to run for the presidency, I rooted for Ralph Nader.

We adjourned to the sitting room and settled him into a comfortable chair, wanting him to do the thing he was struggling not to do. Close his eyes and rest.

Exactly two minutes before I was to walk out the front door, I heard him struggling to find the energy to speak. It must have been hard for him to have kept track of the time so carefully, watching the mantelpiece clock. He began to say something about my plane, then he stopped short.

Immediately, his face turned purple and he was gasping for air. I witnessed my father, the epitome of decorum, swearing like a trooper as he tried to deal with the pain, to breathe. He yelled for his lost dignity. He cursed the loss of his real life. He wanted to die. There in front of me, as if in a cruel game of charades, was my father demonstrating what "crushing" chest pain really is.

He didn't want the medics again, the hospital again, the endless tests, the wretched prognosis, the oxygen tubes. My father, who had scaled mountains, taken jeeps over unchartered desert, fought with the Black Watch in World War Two; my father, who played the mandolin and recited Kipling to his wife, wanted his dignity back.

We called the ambulance. How can you not?

The next day, seeing him in good hands and resting comfortably, I flew back home, planning to return later in the month. After all, he had suffered what the doctors call "neurological events" and "heart problems" for over a year.

Now I am faced with an even bigger guilt than not sitting at that table with him, of getting on that plane. It is that I could have saved his life, but I never found the right words.

It has been almost thirty years since I stopped eating meat and dairy products. Back then, the plaques in my father's arterial walls were just forming. Because I made the switch out of my feelings for animals, I didn't push the health advantages of the diet. My father liked his food too much—from calves' brains on toast to his cholesterol bomb, the breakfast boiled egg—to be swayed away from his old-fashioned "man's man" diet by my stories of mother cows mourning the loss of their infants and tales of the fear you see in all animals' eyes at the slaughterhouse. My mother, wanting to please him, made sure our family larder stocked "real" butter, and that Daddy had his glass of milk in the evenings to help him sleep.

In the later years, during my visits home, my parents tried to appear to have made the switch to vegetarianism, thinking I would stop worrying and nagging. But I found the cans of corned beef tucked away behind the pickles and heard the "slips" in the tales of a newly discovered restaurant that featured veal cordon bleu or chicken curry.

When my father came down with gout, the meat-eater's curse, the jig was up. When he developed prostate trouble, I started in again, sending books on nutrition, giving stern warnings, e-mailing him news articles on the link between heart disease, cancers, and stroke and a meat- and milk-based diet.

By the time the first stroke hit, I knew he wasn't listening. Then came the first heart attack and the loss of circulation in his legs that caused him such pain. My admonitions to chuck the steak for soy fell on deaf ears.

My father believed in God. He believed he was going to see his parents and grandparents and all the wonderful dogs he had loved and walked throughout his life. If his theories about life after death are right, he may be looking down on me as I write this. If he is, I want to say, "Daddy, I'm sorry I didn't get the message. You know I would have stayed at that dining room table and talked forever." I want to tell him, too, that I wish he had gotten my message. If he had, I would be on the phone to him and my mother right now, planning our next picnic at Crater Lake.

❧ *Silence* ❧

DAVID J. CANTOR

The most striking circumstance surrounding my eating only plant-derived foods since August 1989 has been silence. Silence can indicate indifference, but when such a basic matter as the stuff of sustenance is involved, it announces uncommunicated thoughts and feelings. Often it signals determination to avoid outward conflict to preserve a threatened relationship. I hear different content in different people's silence. I base my readings on occasional lapses in the silence—little peeps and squeaks issued from inwardly conflicted minds—and on my knowledge of friends and loved ones from earlier times or other aspects of life.

My next-door neighbor in Glenside, Pennsylvania—a slightly younger adult than me, with a daughter in college, a son in high school, an ex-husband in a nearby state, and a male partner in the neighborhood with two teenage daughters—said to me after my wife and I had lived next door to her for four years, "I'd like to have you guys over for dinner some time, but I don't know how to cook your kind of food." Answering that the food was not a big deal and that we would like to have her over for dinner sometime along with some other neighbors, I kept several "better" answers to myself. "You mean you don't know how to boil a pot of spaghetti or open a bag of potato chips?" for example. Or, "I'm sure most things you cook are free of animal products or can easily be made that way."

Probably due to a long-term snowball effect of custom and habit, advertisements for animal products, and promotions of animal foods dressed up as news or useful diet information, many people think a plant-based diet is exotic. Yet the animals people eat mainly eat plants themselves, and plants are much of what humans eat along with animal parts, secretions, or ova. Replace the chicken of kung pao chicken with tofu, chuck the steak, and double the rice and peas, heat up a couple of soy hot dogs instead of the old-fashioned innards tubes—and you've got it! Yet, apart from my mentioning early on that we are "vegetarian" and apart from my pickup's bumper reading "Meat-Free America" and later "Friends don't let friends eat meat," four years have passed with almost no talk of food between us.

My brother lives three thousand miles away from us with his wife and two daughters. We rarely get together but have a long history of getting along well and having a lot of laughs together. A decade ago, I sent him a book on the advantages to animals, humans, and ecosystems of a plant-based diet and asked for his response, but I never heard anything from him. During my few visits to their home, we discussed food only in mechanical terms. He and I went to a large "health food" store where I could stock up on "my" kind of food. I would eat this, they would eat that. At meal preparation times, little was said. I surmised my brother's wife, whose father hunted deer most of his life and one of whose brothers operates a small farm raising animals for food, particularly wished to avoid discussing ethical aspects of food. They obviously knew what were and were not animal products; no discussion was needed to prevent my being served any. Tall glasses of cow's milk were poured for the girls. All of their meals included some animal-derived foods. Alone on a shelf high up in the pantry closet, I saw the book I had sent my brother, in pristine condition.

One of the few central tenets of our family has always been that no one tells anyone else what to do—a crude version of democracy writ small that has probably resulted in what interpersonal-boundary experts call a boundary violation of too much distance. When my wife and I and my mother and stepfather were due to join my brother's family for Thanksgiving one year in the mid-1990s, I broke the rules. My brother asked me to send a few recipes for main courses, one of which my wife and I would eat while the ten other people at the gathering ate pieces of a turkey. Bowls of vegetables "without butter" would be provided for us while everyone else ate the same vegetables "with butter."

I sent a page from PETA News (I worked at People for the Ethical Treatment of Animals then) that gave plant-based Thanksgiving recipes and, in one column down the side of the page, a description of the horrible existence and mistreatment of turkeys sold for Thanksgiving. I enclosed a note asking if it might be possible for us to have Thanksgiving "without the cooking corpse of a tormented bird filling the house with its stench all day"—something to that effect aimed at suggesting tactlessly that my not eating animal products was not sufficient and that they must not be eaten at all. I felt it necessary to rebel against the silence. In reply, I received an angry letter from my brother that initiated a long correspondence rife with the indignation of people who know and care about each other.

The broader disputes the conflict about food introduced were never resolved; we simply stopped exchanging argumentative letters at some point. In some ways, our relationship is more pleasant than it was before my "turkey corpse" letter disrupted it, and we virtually never discuss food. Occasionally, he is able to visit us when traveling to the East Coast on business. He enjoys the animal-free Chinese carryout I usually pick up. We do not discuss which items to order. I take it that he understands I will not allow any of my money to go toward animal food industries. My brother seems satisfied to have reestablished the silence regarding whether or not to eat animal-derived foods. He allows me to e-mail him information explaining possible dangers of cow's milk and other foods. He usually says nothing in response, though one time in recent memory he thanked me for an article.

A neighbor of ours in our former Arlington, Virginia home was fond of cooking bloody slabs of animal flesh on outdoor charcoal fires—apparently a ritual to help eliminate any possible doubts about his masculinity, since his speaking voice deepened by an octave while he cooked. One day, he told me he would be having a backyard gathering the following weekend and that we were welcome to join him and his friends. I told him we would come and would like to "bring something." That was fine with him: he would not have to concern himself with whether we would "be able to find something to eat."

Silence about food had reigned between us since he and his wife, both hydrogeologists helping manufacturing corporations conform to clean-water laws at minimum cost, had learned we don't eat animals. To the party I brought a large plate heaped with soy hot dogs on rolls, cut in half, with mustard on them— enough servings for a large number of people to have at least one apiece.

Along with meat and cheese and other things people eat who don't limit themselves to fruits, grains, nuts, and vegetables, most of the guests tried the soy hot dogs. A few people said they liked them. Most were silent. The neighbors thanked me for bringing them. I sensed that they hoped a friendly comment would forestall any lecture I might be thinking of delivering to their friends about the evils of "meat."

Sure, I have used many opportunities to inform people of animals' rights, the cruelty inherent in animal food production, of animals' possessing much greater mental lives than is often assumed, of the damage to the environment from factory farming, of the benefits to human health of a plants-only diet, of the fiction that sufficient protein can only be obtained from animal foods, and other information that one would think would be more than enough to end the use of animals for food. I have published many letters about those things, provided people with articles and books and web addresses, and answered questions. But only a few people have ever told me they stopped purchasing any animal foods, let alone all animal foods, due to the information I provided. Those few are people who approached me about food choices—I did not approach them— and were particularly interested and open to the possibility that they might wish to make new choices.

In addition to the possibility that I am not very good at broaching such matters, I believe other powerful factors are at work. People associate particular foods with religious rituals, beliefs about how to have good times, how one perpetuates family customs, what it is to be a good parent, how to ensure that one is seen as belonging to a particular peer group or profession, how to appear "normal," and other values.

Such associations have developed through misplaced priorities, but they have become important to many people in the way shoes are to Imelda Marcos. I have always valued independence of thought, and as long as I can remember I have believed action must follow thought and people must base choices on the most important relevant facts in order to maintain integrity and self-respect and to enjoy life to the utmost while doing the least harm. I often feel sorry for people who enslave themselves to destructive social fictions and seek to convince themselves that doing so enriches their lives.

My feelings alone, however, do little to liberate animals from the vast, noisy, unfeeling animal-food machine that grinds on day after day spitting out once-living, conscious beings into Styrofoam™ packages, cans, cooking pots, broilers, and ultimately people's hapless bodies. Food choices, despite their political aspects, are typically seen as personal choices, so commenting on them without invitation is often perceived as violating personal boundaries. Those who enjoy eating meat get to act offended and to exempt themselves from considering relevant facts.

The people I describe in this essay are very nice—much nicer than me, some of them. Our society is first and foremost a violent one in which being nice is consistent with partaking of the fruits of violence wrought by society as a whole. It required the destruction of millions of innocent people to occupy so much of North America. It has required the needless destruction of countless thousands more in serving our own perceived interests. We have passed on many opportunities to help others or to reverse damage we have done, while also in some instances acting so as to rescue, restore justice, heal, and improve the quality of life. Our society has enormously accelerated the rate at which and the extent to which human beings reap short-term gain and long-term harm at the expense of other beings and entire ecosystems. Little public discourse takes place regarding ethical and political aspects of consumer choices. That would violate the "buying mood" advertisers insist entertainment media maintain. Millions and millions of nice people populate "our" continent, and it would surely be a much more difficult place in which to live if people were not so nice. Being nice, though, is distinct from exploring consequences of one's actions and adjusting them accordingly. It seems to assume only local, immediately visible consequences need be considered. Being nice may even entail disregarding ethical aspects of things so as to avoid open conflict or danger. As Lou Reed says, "The goodly hearted made lampshades and soap." That doesn't mean nice people aren't nice, though.

Heads of large, horned animals killed by hunters in Africa look down from all four walls on diners at Ruth's Chris Steakhouse on Broad Street in Philadelphia, where I found myself feasting on potatoes, salad, and some of the best-prepared broccoli I had ever tasted. My wife's aunt had given her children and their spouses gift certificates to that restaurant, and they invited us to join them for the big meal. My memory still reverberates with the cousins' exclamations of how good the "surf 'n' turf" was, how tender the "T-bone." I don't know these relatives extremely well, but they are a competitive bunch, often comparing their purchases in good-natured one-upsmanship. In solidarity with my long-lost animal relatives up there on the walls, it was my turn to be silent.

❧ *Becoming Vegetarian Again* ❧
DILIP BARMAN

Nowadays, in Canada and the U. S., it isn't hard to run into people of Indian descent, particularly in mid- and large-sized towns. However, in 1959 or 1960, when my parents emigrated from India to the U. S., there were very few people here from the subcontinent.

I was born in Philadelphia, where my dad had come to get a graduate degree, and my mom told me stories about having to travel to New York City just to get Indian spices and groceries! Later, in small town Ohio, where my dad was lured by an enticing job offer, I was embraced by an Italian grandmother, our landlady, and my mom's delicious and "exotic" Indian cooking garnered her an article in the local newspaper for a friendly and curious audience, who probably had never heard of a samosa or curry.

Though both sides of my Hindu family come from a long line of vegetarians, when I was quite young my parents exposed me to the eating of dead animals. I don't know why—maybe it was for pragmatic reasons: to help ensure I would fit in to this new country, to give me a diverse diet so I could easily eat out when older, or because of the loving and well-intentioned desires of my new Italian "grandmother," calling me ("manga, manga!") to share dinners with her (my mom learned from her how to make great pizza!). I've since found out that my story is not so atypical among Indian immigrants, at least Hindus—Jains seem in overwhelming numbers not to succumb.

To be sure, it was clear to me that meat-eating was aberrant behavior. For many Hindus, *ahimsa* (or non-harm) dictates that animals are not to be eaten for ethical and compassionate reasons, but also because there is a sense of the impure or unclean in even touching dead flesh, akin perhaps to Jewish kosher rules about food. My parents would sometimes take me to fast food restaurants like McDonald's, White Castle Hamburgers, and a local one with curb-service, Dog and Suds. They would watch while I ate the meal, then instruct me to wash my hands and lips with soap. Once in a while, we would bring take-out home; my mother would spread newspapers on the floor, and I would eat there, disposing (this is before the days of recycling!) the paper afterwards.

Though my mom is a strict lacto-vegetarian (she doesn't even eat onions or garlic, though that's a totally different story), most Hindu vegetarians seem to be "eggitarians," meaning they will eat dairy products but not eggs, but they may very well eat eggs non-explicitly, such as when included in prepared cakes, cookies, and desserts. Given this less taboo status of eggs, my mother, amazingly to me now, would actually once in a while make a go of making scrambled eggs, hard-boiled eggs, or an omelet for me. She kept an entirely different frying pan and set of utensils, and even a separate portable electric range. I can't remember, but strongly suspect that she did the cooking on the floor and that I ate on the floor.

I hope that I'm perceived as tolerant, particularly when I speak to the public and try to make new members welcome in our vegetarian society. Life is difficult and, though I strongly believe in the importance of veganism and vegetarianism in general, I can understand how easy it is for one to justify one's choices. My older siblings and aunt would criticize me for eating meat. I remember my aunts making impassioned arguments about how innocent animals were being killed just for my palate, and my dismissing her with references to carnivorous animals in the jungles (without understanding obvious points such as that we may be omnivorous, but study of our teeth and digestive system shows we're more akin to herbivores; and that in modern society, meat-eating is totally unnecessary and causes such environmental destruction, to speak nothing about effects on human health and the mistreatment of animals).

Though my meat-eating was relatively rare, it increased in frequency in the second half of high school when I worked at McDonald's and then the first year of college with dormitory food. For me, meat was something different than what we ate at home, and I probably saw it as a treat, maybe like I see going out for dhosa now. (Dhosa is one of my favorite foods—it's a south Indian crepe filled with savory vegetables, and—at least so far— I can't make it very well myself!)

My story comes to a happy end when I went to college. I attended a university where dormitories were only provided for freshmen. I had to find an apartment for myself after that first year and start cooking for myself. I remember going grocery shopping for the first time when I was on my own, and coming upon the meat section. It hit me—these were dead animals, and they had been forced to give their lives just so I could eat them.

I was still unaware of just how horrible their lives probably had been, and hadn't heard the term "factory farming," but I was still moved by the unfairness of it, as well as the disgusting and sad appearance of packaged slabs of flesh. It's very different, at least for me, eating prepared non-vegetarian food and having to stare and come to terms with raw meat—I still can't understand how my non-vegetarian friends can easily handle chicken and turkey carcasses, or any meat.

That trip to the grocery store launched me almost immediately on a return to my family's roots and voluntarily embrace vegetarianism. It was the beginning of a journey to become ovo-lacto vegetarian (I would make scrambled eggs—and remember to wash my hands and lips with soap afterwards!), then lacto (I don't think I ever was eggitarian). Since becoming involved with vegetarian organizations, I've learned about the problems with dairy, and in recent years have become a near-vegan.

I hope that in some little way this story might be of interest to fellow vegetarians. Maybe it will remind you that you may not always have felt or understood the realities behind what it takes to bring dead animals to the table. I hope that it will strengthen your tolerance of others and, while you should feel good about doing your part to make available factual information about compassionate living or even just being a model of how easy and healthy a vegetarian diet is to follow, it will have increased your understanding that people need to come to self-realization. If you are new to Canada or the U. S. and come from a culture that has a strong focus on vegetarianism, I hope you will look around and see the tremendous strides we've made so that there is little, if any, difficulty fitting in most places as a vegetarian.

Italian Vegetarian
ILARIA FERRI

I was born in the ancient city of Rome, on 23 March 1968, and I still live in Italy. When I was very young, I had the fantastic opportunity of living during the holidays in a farm belonging to my mother's uncle in Tuscany, one of the most beautiful regions of Italy. When I was twelve, my family and I moved to the country, where I lived near animals, growing up like a little "human-animal."

I spent my time looking at the pigs playing with each other, noticing how the cows were sweet with their calves, how the ducks were funny with all their ducklings following in single file! I picked up many stray cats and dogs during my life, and I understand how they can be happy and how they are able to transmit their love and their gratitude.

This was perhaps the reason I have decided to become a veterinarian and to dedicate my life trying to obtaining respect, care, and rights for all the animals. I have also discovered the incredible world of the sea and have decided to be a vet for marine mammals. I'm still studying dolphins and I'm working very hard for an international organization named Animal and Nature Conservation Fund to get them freed from captivity.

There aren't, for me, animals one eats or animals you love. Animals are animals and they must be respected. My grandmother always used to tell me that my respect for animals was something innate for me. I used to scold my relatives if they didn't see the ants on the floor or the snails on the grass and they crushed them! I was also saddened by the fact my father was a hunter and sometimes I saw him return home with the poor birds and ducks he had killed.

I started to have problems with him and with my family because I didn't accept the eating of animals, any sort of animals. I would say, "my dog is my friend, the cow is my friend. I don't want to eat my friends!" When I was fifteen, I summoned the will to say "*No more*." My mother was very important during this period in my life, because she understood me and started to respect my thoughts even if the rest of the family called her insane and unreasonable!

What is really interesting, I think, is to try and understand how difficult it is to be vegetarian and vegan in Italy and to see the behavior of the common people if you don't accept steak or meat or fish etc. You can't normally eat in a restaurant. I think the situation will improve, as there are vegetarian restaurants in the big Italian cities. And there should be here in Italy many dishes without animals because, in our old culture, when we were much poorer than now, common people used to eat lentils or beans with pasta and potatoes and other vegetables.

What most Italians don't have is the culture of respect. Normally, we don't respect each other, so you can imagine what it would mean for us to respect the animals!

While some things may have changed over the last twenty years of the struggle for animal rights, it is still very hard to be an advocate for animals. You have to be strong and full of passion; you have to have a group of vegetarian friends—because you can be made to feel so abnormal. You need to have human relationships; because sometimes people call you "mad" or an "extremist."

I had problems with my doctors, because they said that every illness I got was because I am a vegetarian. I had problems at school because I couldn't eat in the school cafeteria and had to bring my lunch from home. I had problems with my teachers because they didn't accept or respect my "insane behavior."

I don't have those problems now, but they were huge problems when I was a teenager. I was very depressed and I felt so alone and unappreciated. But, thanks to my therapist, I realized at twenty-four years old that the pain and ridicule I felt could become my energy and my force. This is how I became what I am.

Now I speak with all types of people. I know that some of them will understand sooner or later the sense of life: *respect*. I truly believe that the human race needs to discover the joy that we can have helping, loving, but especially respecting the animals in all their different sizes and shapes and personalities.

❧ *Transition to a Vegetarian Lifestyle* ❧
JUSTIN SIVEY

The year was 1996, and I was a sophomore at a university in Colorado. I was about to have my life changed for the good, forever.

Following what I had been taught for years, I was the typical meat-and-potatoes boy, as mostly everybody else who walked the halls with me was. Walking to class one day, I noticed a flyer advertising a talk by a philosophy professor on animal rights put on by the animal rights group on campus. I had always had an interest in animal treatment, including being somewhat familiar with People for the Ethical Treatment of Animals. Walking into the room that afternoon, I was shocked by the turnout. Every group of people, from cowboys to hippies, was present. I was excited.

As the talk progressed, I became aware of the goal the professor was trying to accomplish—to illustrate the never-before-thought-of premise that even some cowboys care for how "their" animals are treated. Obviously, I don't necessarily agree with this, but some in the room did, as basically the premise rested on the fact that no one would treat badly a commodity of theirs that was worth money. Barring any further critique of this premise, the talk was nonetheless extremely mind-opening. It was incredible to see such a concern with these issues, as well as to hear points that I had never been exposed to before.

A few weeks later, I again saw a flyer for an event put on by the campus animal rights group. Jan Hamilton, the director of Wilderness Ranch Sanctuary for Farm Animals, came to speak for the group. Jan spoke mostly of the plight of what are considered food animals as well as her incredible organization, one that provides sanctuary for those individuals lucky enough to escape such situations. It all made sense to me. I remember feeling so weird in my newly purchased leather shoes. Here I was agreeing with Jan, but at the same time I was wearing the skin of one of those she was speaking for. I left with much to think about.

Feeling the gates of awareness open up, I began to feel and think like a different person. I still hadn't entirely changed my eating habits, mostly because I still at that point did not know what was truly going on behind the production of the meat, dairy, eggs, etc. that I was eating and wearing. I needed that one final push. It came two weeks later when I saw another flyer, this one advertising a talk by PETA co-founder, Alex Pacheco. "Wow," I thought. I knew his name and who he was, and I couldn't believe he was coming to our campus. I couldn't wait.

The night came. This time, as I entered the large lecture hall, I was totally blown away. There must have been 300 people packed into the room, an even larger assortment of people than at both talks before. I couldn't believe the interest. Alex was introduced and briefly spoke. He mentioned that he would begin the evening with a video, followed by a speech of about forty-five minutes.

The room went dark. A few coughs were heard, as well as the squeaking of chairs. "A movie," I thought. "This should be interesting." And then it began. The movie opened up with a scene of a fox caught in a steel trap. In a state of panic, the fox was gnawing at his leg, trying desperately to get himself free. The movie went on. Graphic, true-life scenes of cows being strung up by their legs, still alive, and being skinned. Animals in testing facilities having chemicals dropped into their eyes as they squirmed and screamed for mercy. And the scene that I will remember forever: a pig being burned alive with a blowtorch, kicking and twitching on the ground in pure pain and agony.

The movie went on like this. Suddenly, it stopped. The light went on. This time, the sounds heard were very different. The coughing and squeaking of chairs were replaced with loud sobs of tears and quiet mumbling about the horrors just witnessed. I personally had to restrain myself from jumping from my seat and, in a fit of rage, doing something to something or someone.

Alex spoke. He spoke of the truth of the video, and the necessity of action that must be taken to address these very real, and very desperate issues. He spoke of courage and the need for us to stand up to these atrocities and change our lives. He spoke of the need for those of us who can speak, to speak for those who can't.

As I look back on that night, I realize that Alex Pacheco was the most influential person of my life. After the video and his talk, my talk had to turn to action. I had always loved animals, but I hadn't realized the hypocrisy of that statement if I was not a vegetarian. I changed my life completely. I threw away my leather shoes. I bought only animal-free and non–animal-tested products. I went vegan. I read everything I could about these issues, growing with each new line I read. But most importantly, after leaving university that semester, and enrolling at another university, I started an animal rights club; the first ever on the Auraria campus in Denver, Colorado.

It hasn't been easy. People are pretty apathetic. But I have been able to distribute some good information to people who otherwise would have never had the opportunity to see it, and that's more than if I hadn't had started the club at all. But I'm hoping to have that one very important person, Alex Pacheco, come to our campus and do what he did for my life, to the lives of others. Nobody is better at it than him. We'll hope it happens.

That change, and that person saved my life. Going down the path of ignorance, one can never truly be free. Alex Pacheco exposed me to the truth, a truth that I never knew existed. Ignorance may be bliss, but it's not the truth. And the truth—well, nothing is more perfect or liberating than the truth. I have never looked back.

Although I never truly cared what my family or friends thought (and, yes, I did lose most of my friends), it was hard to constantly explain myself to them. But when I start to feel the discomfort or stress from such ignorant comments, or have to deal with living in a meat-eating society, I always remember one thing: the momentary discomfort that I feel from those situations could never even compare to the pain that that pig felt when he was burned alive with a blow torch. That's all I have to remember. The discomfort quickly changes to motivation and inspiration to do something to help stop atrocities like that one. That is all that matters.

❧ *A Bag of Raw Flesh* ❧
AMANDA PANKIW

I grew up on a farm in rural Saskatchewan, Canada. We raised cattle, chickens, and pigs. Every night for dinner we would have meat. Growing up I knew that animals had a personality and feelings from watching our animals. Our family loved our animals, but still some of them ended up on our dinner table.

When I moved away from home, I didn't eat as much meat because it was so expensive and I couldn't afford it on my small budget. I'd always thought of becoming a vegetarian and once in a while I would stop eating meat altogether, but I would always go back to it.

Then, one day, I was doing my weekly grocery shopping. That week the store that I shopped at was having a meat sale. They gave the customers a big brown bag to fill up with meat and then the customer would get ten percent off. The sight of this made me sick to my stomach. A big bag of raw flesh. All of these people wheeling their carts around with bags of flesh in them. I quickly got the rest of the things that I needed and got out of there.

On my drive home I thought about how wrong it was to eat animals. There are so many alternatives available to us. I started doing some research on the internet and at a bookstore. I visited the website of People for the Ethical Treatment of Animals (PETA). It showed pictures of the conditions animals often live in and it made me cry. That day I decided to become a vegan.

It was difficult at first and I even had one backslide. But I found an awesome cookbook called *How It All Vegan*. In it, there are easy to make recipes and great tips.

The greatest challenge though remains eating out. Sometimes the only thing that I can get is fries, but when I think about it, it's all worth it.

❧ *The Decision* ❧

LAURIE CRAWFORD STONE

Sixteen years ago, I awakened one April morning and decided the previous night's grilled steak was my last. I had been considering becoming a vegetarian for several years and it was time to get serious. For years, I had been listening to my sister and brother tell me why I shouldn't eat meat or wear animal hides. My sister, Jan Crawford, was an early vegetarian in our Midwestern city of Cedar Rapids, Iowa. Jan was not confrontational about her choice but would make efforts to educate her four siblings and suggest alternative meal choices whenever the opportunity arose. I will never forget the difficulty she had ordering food in restaurants and even getting her family members to remember and respect her choice. One time I, unthinkingly, served a dip that had deviled ham as an ingredient—my poor unsuspecting sister ate it and immediately became physically ill.

My brother, Dave Crawford, co-founder and executive director of Rocky Mountain Animal Defense, was the next vegetarian in our family. Dave, our brother Bruce, and I had all worked at a slaughterhouse in Cedar Rapids in the late 1970s. I hired my two younger brothers to work there. Bruce was lucky. He worked on the loading dock and saw none of the atrocities that Dave and I witnessed. I was hired initially in a human resources position that meant I had to walk through the slaughterhouse on occasion. The first time I appeared on the "kill" floor, an employee threw a cow's tongue at me as I stared horrified at the cows being stunned and then shot through the forehead with a slug. Nothing prepared me for the sight of those huge beautiful animals slumping in immediate death. Equally upsetting was seeing hogs break away and running wildly, trying to escape the conveyor belt that carried them up one floor to their death. Their screaming is a sound I will never forget.

Shortly after being killed, the animal's heads were severed from their bodies. Hundreds of bodyless heads were attached to hooks on a conveyor belt and moved through the plant like so many widgets. But they weren't widgets. These were animals that had been alive only minutes before.

The bodies of pigs were dipped to remove their hair. Cows were skinned and their hides were taken to the hide cellar—a cold, damp basement where the hides were laid out and treated to prepare them for manufacturing leather clothing and other items.

It was amazing how quickly the work to dissemble the animal's bodies occurred. It seemed a race to remove any semblance to a living being. No wonder many of the employees who worked on the "kill" spent their breaks and lunch hour at a nearby bar trying to forget the morning and numb themselves for their afternoon's work.

I have seen "downers." These are the animals who have been injured and cannot walk to their death. These cows and pigs are left in the yard in all kinds of weather, often all day. They are then killed or their already dead bodies are dragged off to the rendering area of the plant. This is the area where the otherwise unused animal body parts are cooked and dried to make products like blood meal. The clothing I wore on visits to this area was thrown away when I left the slaughterhouse for good. The stench could not be washed away.

After he left "The Pack" (employer and employees called this a meat-packing plant rather than slaughterhouse), Dave converted to vegetarianism. He is now a vegan. Dave was and remains diligent about converting others. Dave's conversion had a great impact on me—largely because he and I shared the slaughterhouse experience. I was the last sibling to convert. Although none of us quit eating meat for health reasons, we have reaped health benefits. My other relatives struggle with high cholesterol and other health issues.

Negative and Positive Reactions

Converting to vegetarianism was the easy part. I have been amazed by the range of reactions by others to me and my decision. Fortunately, through my animal work and social contacts, I have met some like-minded people who have been vegetarians for years—some for health reasons and some for humane reasons. Some of my friends have recently reduced or eliminated meat consumption. Others ask why I don't eat meat and seem genuinely interested in the reasons. Some people refuse to respect the choice and serve meat-dominated dishes at parties and social functions. These folks still think a raw vegetable platter and chips are an acceptable buffet meal for vegetarians. Others seem threatened and are confrontational. I find that people who are confrontational about the meat/animal exploitation issue have a general disregard for animals and animal lives. Some examples follow.

Shortly after converting, I read during a flight to Atlanta the horrors that produce veal. That night I had dinner with my boss and his wife and several other people. I was appalled when my boss's wife said she was going to order veal. Still new to this and fairly naive, I told her about veal calves being separated from their mothers at birth, kept in small crates in the dark so they wouldn't develop muscles, and having chronic diarrhea from being fed only milk. I thought she would change her mind. Not only did she order veal, she told me she didn't care about the calves. And, as though I had just thrown down a glove, her husband, laughing, shared the story of how they had neutered their cat themselves one night while drunk.

Another adamant meat-eater loudly announced that he wanted veal or lamb when I was nearby. I think he thought he was being funny, since he wouldn't have ordered those items if I had been at the same table, though he and others were likely to have ordered a hamburger. His wife was incredulous upon learning last year that I rescued a litter of kittens from a wood-pile. She reported that her family used to drown farm kittens.

Recently, my husband and I hosted a gourmet dinner for three other couples. The dinner had been purchased at a fund-raising auction. The donor chefs were two couples who are well-traveled and love to eat at fine restaurants. They consider themselves to be connoisseurs of fine foods and wines. I reminded the chefs on several occasions prior to the date (one has known me for fifteen years) that I don't eat meat and asked them to please plan the meal accordingly. We arrived at the beautiful home of one of the chefs and were immediately offered wine and appetizers. There were two wonderful non-meat choices. I was hopeful! Although I am not a large woman, I do love to eat and had been looking forward to this evening for some time. I had eaten only a small breakfast and lunch. We were soon seated at an interesting custom-designed table. The first course salad was served atop prosciutto (an Italian bacon). I felt I could forgive this as my salad was delivered minus the prosciutto. I wrongly assumed they had decided to serve just this one meat item. The main course was brought out on individual plates. My friend's plates contained some sort of beef roast stuffed with more prosciutto, and potatoes and green beans. When it arrived, my plate contained one slice of eggplant (which I loathe), potatoes, and green beans. I figured I was still okay. I could eat the potatoes and green beans and feel satisfied. Imagine my surprise when I put my fork into the potatoes and found them layered with onion and more bacon! All of us were shocked by the meal. Even the meat-eaters felt they had eaten too much meat! Meanwhile, our hosts and chefs were dining contentedly on this same food in the kitchen. These same couples have told stories of purchasing live lobsters and having lobster races and other "games" before boiling them to death.

Over the years, I have tempered what I volunteer in social situations about eating animals. I find that most people do not want to know the conditions under which animals live and die for human consumption. On rare occasions, I am asked for details, but mostly people want to discuss vegetarianism from the standpoint of health benefits. Occasionally, when new information about animals or animal products is made public, I am asked for details. Since the goal is to end the consumption of meat and other animal products, I believe any reason is a good one!

Several friends have changed their diets recently. One dear friend has reduced her meat consumption after being diagnosed with breast cancer. She believes that food choices had a role in causing her disease and will be a major factor in her recovery.

Another friend changed his diet drastically after being diagnosed
with diabetes. Yet another friend changed after having a high
cholesterol reading. Another friend has been reading about milk
and other animal products. She is asking for healthy choices for
her five children.

My husband has greatly changed his eating habits. Education
and respect for my beliefs were key to his decision to reduce his
meat consumption. He was raised in a meat-for-every-meal rural
Iowa family. He still eats meat occasionally when we are out. His
reasons for reduced meat consumption are both health and
humanely motivated. He believes that those who don't exploit
animals are the wave of the future. That supportive attitude has
been expressed to others.

We recently had dinner with Iowa Governor Tom Vilsack
and his wife. Governor Vilsack promotes Iowa as the Food
Capital of the world. Unfortunately, most of the current food
production here is factory farming of eggs, poultry, and hogs.
Iowa has the second largest egg production (thus, hens) in the
United States. My husband had called ahead and requested a
vegetarian meal for me. During dinner, the Governor asked
about my portobello mushroom served amid thirteen plates of
pork hocks. I explained that I am a vegetarian and that the decision had been made after working in an Iowa slaughterhouse
years ago. I told him that I had seen how meat is processed and
had even sold meat to grocery stores. He responded that I probably knew more than they did about what they were eating. I
agreed. He expressed surprise that I get enough to eat without
meat. He was curious about what I eat instead of meat. I gave
him some examples. When he still appeared unconvinced, my

husband interjected that he often eats meatless meals and is satisfied with the alternatives!

A Victory and the Future

I suspect one of the gourmet dinner chefs mentioned above was responsible for duck foie gras appearing on the New Year's Eve menu at a local club. The menu was announced in early December, 2000. I immediately contacted Lisa Lange, a friend at People for the Ethical Treatment of Animals, and requested materials. When the written materials and video arrived, I called the club manager and requested a meeting. I told him I had some information about foie gras that I hoped he would look at or let me explain. He asked me to go ahead and tell him about it. I explained that foie gras is produced by force feeding ducks and geese large amounts of grain through a metal tube, that their livers are horribly enlarged from being fed unnaturally large amounts of food all at once, that their throats are damaged so they are unable to eat normally, and that workers receive a bonus if they kill "only" fifty birds a month. I requested that foie gras be removed from the New Year's Eve menu. He seemed shocked by what I told him. He told me he had no idea this was how foie gras was produced and asked if this was how geese foie gras was also produced. I told him it was. I delivered the materials to him later that same day. The following evening, I saw the manager at dinner. He came to our table and told me they had removed the foie gras from the New Year's Eve menu! This meant 300 servings of duck foie gras were not purchased!

As I learn more about how animal derived products are produced, I continue to eliminate animal products from my diet. I am moving toward veganism. Friends are more open to vegetarian and vegan diets as they face health issues brought on by age and lifestyle choices. I believe the trend will be to reduce consumption of animals and the products derived from their exploitation.

❧ *Veggie Tale* ❧
HEATHER FARR

It hasn't been long that I've been a vegetarian...only a few years. I certainly didn't come from a vegetarian background. When I was growing up there wasn't a food pyramid. We went by the four food groups: fruit, vegetables, grains, and meat. Every meal contained something from each group and you didn't leave the table until you cleaned your plate. Up until I moved out to go to college I ate meat at least twice a day.

I didn't become a vegetarian when I left for school; I just changed my eating habits. Instead of the four food groups, sometimes a meal consisted of a can of pop and a candy bar; other times it was chicken wings or burgers. I never gave meat on my plate a second thought—that is until several years later. I had stumbled into a job at a humane society. We mostly dealt with cats and dogs. But, every now and then, we had animals that didn't fall into either of these categories. It is one of these animal that brought me to see things in a whole new light.

We had a pig at the shelter. I don't remember how this first one came to us, we had several over the years. But I remember he wasn't at all what I had expected. I thought that a pig was a grunting, dirty animal that ate slop and rolled in the mud. I remember how surprised I was to touch him for the first time. I expected him to be soft like a baby's bottom. I suppose that I thought this because of what the pigs always look like in cartoons and storybooks. Instead he was rough with very coarse hairs sticking out. Not only did it physically feel different than I had imagined but he also felt (emotionally) different than I had imagined. He had a personality. He reacted to different things and different people much like a dog would. I began to look forward to seeing him every morning. I believe that he felt the same about myself and my colleagues.

Because we weren't set up to take this type of animal we had to keep him in a run in the dog room. It was extremely noisy with all the dogs barking every time someone came into the room, and I'm sure it was quite unsettling for the little pig. But it didn't get him down. Anytime he heard a familiar voice he would hurry to the front of his run and make all sorts of noise to get your attention. If I let him out he would follow me anywhere I went. We managed to find a harness for him and would take him out for walks on a leash. He loved to be rubbed and would roll over when he was ready for a belly rub. It didn't take long for him to figure out that he got attention when he made a ruckus. So if he was in his run and you were in earshot he would make the most awful noise to get you to come running. I'd have terrible thoughts that something awful had happened and as soon as he saw me he was as happy as can be. He'd wag his tail and give me that "works every time" look. I had to laugh at his antics. He longed to be in the company of people and would squirm and struggle when you walked him back to his run. It became a game and sometimes quite a challenge.

It didn't take long to bond with this little guy. In fact I wanted so desperately to make him a permanent part of my life. If I had been able, I would have brought him home. It still brings a smile to my face when I think of his piggy kisses and lovable personality. I was sad to see him go but also ecstatic that he was going where he would be a pet, not just a pig.

I owe a lot to this pig. When he first came into the shelter the joke was that we were going to have a pig roast at the end of the summer. Looking back I am ashamed to admit that. And after spending just a little time with this living, breathing, and, most importantly, feeling creature, I would never even consider such a horrific thought. Because of him I began to sit down to a meal and realize that it wasn't just "meat" on my plate but a creature that had feelings and personality, that if given the opportunity could bring joy to someone's life. I lost my appetite for meat and became a vegetarian. I know that if people were able to have similar experiences and get to know who they were eating, there would be a lot more of us veggies out there!

❧ *Contributors* ❧

Maryanne Appel

Maryanne lives in Boothwyn, Pennsylvania with her husband and three vegan companion animals; two dogs and a rabbit. She is a member of several animal rights organizations, supports a dozen or more animal sanctuaries, and participates in various vegan outreach programs. She recently completed an article on vegan cats and dogs which was published in the newsletter of a local animal rights organization.

Ilse Marie Baca

Ilse Marie was born in New Mexico, two days before Christmas 1974. In 1992, she studied Communication and English Literature at a small liberal arts college in New Mexico, where she was active in college radio and newspaper. In 1996, she was living in Santa Fe, where she tried to start a rock and roll band, while studying Oriental Medicine. The call of rock and roll beckoned, though, and she moved to Los Angeles. In 1999, her first year in California, Ilse became immersed in the animal rights movement while working for a local (nationwide) animal rights group. It was then she decided to become vegan, after having been a vegetarian for eight years. Ilse currently is working with internet radio stations and other corporate entities, while surrounding herself with all things alive, electric, and inspiring.

Dilip Barman

Dilip is President of the Triangle Vegetarian Society (TVS), based in North Carolina. He has been a vegetarian advocate for many years and has appeared on local and national television on topics such as trends in vegetarianism, vegan Thanksgivings, and the dangers of irradiated foods. In addition to his organization's newsletter, Dilip has published cooking articles in a number of books and newspapers and has taught vegetarian cooking classes for several organizations. His website is: www.trianglevegsociety.org

Susan S. Barber

Susan has been a vegan and animal rights activist since 1996. 25-year old Susan has worked with the Humane Society as one of their District Captains in the Humane Activist Network, in addition to working for human rights in Tibet. She is deeply involved with Green politics. She helped organize Ralph Nader's presidential campaign in 2000 and is currently the Secretary of the Arizona Green Party. Susan earned her B.A. in Women's Studies from Arizona State University in 1999 and plans to attend law school in order to pursue a career as an animal rights/public interest attorney. When not pursuing activist concerns, Susan enjoys crochet, bicycling, reading, and public speaking. She is president of her local Toastmasters Club.

David J. Cantor

David has worked full time in the animal rights movement since August of 1989. He has published many articles and letters on behalf of other-than-human animals.

Diana Cox

Diana is an English teacher in one of the tertiary institutions in Hong Kong. Before that she worked at the British Council. She has also taught English in Madrid and in Rome. She is English but has lived outside England for over twelve years. Vegetarianism led her to an interest in animal rights. Her degree is in philosophy and she's interested in the philosophical/ethical arguments as well as in the practical, commonsensical ones. Hong Kong has an active vegan society which meets every month to eat out. There is also a vegetarian society. Most of the vegetarian restaurants here are Chinese or Indian. There are very few Western ones (only one as far as she knows), but Diana is pleased to report that the number of vegetarians in Hong Kong is growing.

Diana Engoron

Diane is forty-four years old and has been happily married for sixteen years to another animal lover and animal rights activist. She presently resides in New York, but is planning a move to New Zealand to pursue a simple and natural life. She hopes to someday own her own mini-farm to care for unwanted and unloved animals.

Brian Evans

Born in Philadelphia, PA, Brian graduated from Temple University in Mathematics Education, with a bachelor and masters degree. He is currently in the doctoral program for Mathematics Education at Temple. He has been an animal rights activist since 1994.

Heather Farr

Heather grew up in western New York. She met her then future husband Kenn while attending college in Alfred, New York. They moved to Elmira, New York after they married, where she began volunteering at the local humane society and was soon offered a job. Along with that came her first rescued animal and a move to Pine City. Heather states, "We are the only people I know who bought their house for the dog." Several years and pets later she is once again a pet lover, something she has been all her life. But now she is also a vege-tarian thanks to her friends. Heather resides in Pine City with Kenn and their daughter Cameron. They love spending time with their dog Chloe and cat Muffin as well as all of the "just passing through" wildlife that visits their acreage.

Marion Friedman

Marion was born in Philadelphia, Pennsylvania in 1924. She has resided in Philadelphia her entire life. She was raised in a Jewish orphanage from the ages of four to eighteen, where a night nurse was her inspiration to adopt a vegetarian diet. She was the only child in the orphanage who was a vegetarian. Over a twenty-one-year period, Marion attended night classes, majoring in German language and literature. She graduated from the University of Pennsylvania in 1981 at the age of fifty-seven. She studied interpretive (modern) dance and, while in her early sixties, appeared in a University of Pennsylvania employee show as a group dancer.

Lee Hall

Lee has recently co-authored an article in the format of a U. S. Supreme Court brief. The plaintiff is a nonhuman ape named Evelyn Hart. This is the first appearance in a North American law review of a model brief that argues for the emancipation of nonhumans under anti-slavery amendments to the Constitution. It will be useful to lawyers who work for the first cases to extend actual rights to nonhuman beings. The article was used by Reenie Marx, a teacher in Canada, who offered a semester-long course in which students did the legal research and preparation for a mock trial. The event was covered on the Internet and by the *Montreal Gazette*.

Rebekah Harp

Rebekah is a special education teacher in Jacksonville, Florida. She attended Wesleyan College and graduated from the University of Georgia with a psychology degree. She also received a teaching degree from the University of North Florida. Rebekah was named "Teacher of the Year" at her elementary school in 1996, and in 2000 she was honored by the Jacksonville Humane Society as "Humane Educator of the Year." She created Jacksonville's first student-based "Junior Humane

Society" in 1999 and continues its implementation in other schools. Rebekah shares her home with six cats and three dogs, all companion animals who were former strays or rescues. Although most of her companions still choose a carnivorous lifestyle, her dogs Delia, Madeline, and Leonardo have learned to love tofu shakes and veggie burgers!

Jean Lauren

Jean is a retired registered nurse. She was an army nurse during World War II, stationed in Verdeen, France. In her early forties, she became more sensitive to the issues of animal cruelty and, as she began to realize the connection to her lifestyle, gradually changed to a vegetarian diet. She has been a vegan for twenty years.

Jeff Lydon

Jeff is a writer and animal advocate living in the woods of central New York's Finger Lakes region with his wife, Sarah, and their dog, Quinn. For his day job, Jeff directs the local Head Start program.

Erik Marcus

Erik is the publisher of Vegan.com. This passage is excerpted from his book: *Vegan: The New Ethics of Eating* (McBooks Press 2000, www.vegan.com)

Jennie Taylor Martin

Jennie works for People for the Ethical Treatment of Animals (PETA).

Johanna McCloy

Johanna became a vegan in November 1999. In June 2000, she founded "Soy Happy!" a campaign to get veggie dogs added to Major League Baseball stadiums and other large venues throughout the U. S. and Canada. The campaign has been very successful. In addition, Johanna is the content director for MoviesThatMatter.com, a site about movies with a social conscience and actor activists making a difference. Johanna freelances as a writer with personal essays published in various magazines and a one-act play possibly to be produced in Los Angeles. Among her professional acting credits is the role of Ensign Calloway in "Star Trek: The Next Generation." Currently, Johanna is working on a television documentary series she created and plans to produce, entitled "Earth Angels." She resides with her boyfriend and their menagerie of animals in Los Angeles. For more information about "Soy Happy!" visit www.soyhappy.org.

Lesa Miller
Lesa is a receptionist/humane educator at The Fund for Animals, Silver Spring, MD.

Rochelle Mitchell
Rochelle has been vegetarian for six years. She lives in New England with her husband and their three children. Her poems have appeared in several small magazines. Her poem, "My Forever Child," received honorable mention in the First Annual Mandy Poetry Contest.

Erin Moore
Erin was born in the San Francisco Bay Area, where she lived until she left for Oregon State University in 1994. She's been vegan since 1998, and has not once wished she wasn't. She is a grad student in Atmospheric Science at OSU, and also got her B.S. in math there. When people ask her what she's going to do in the future, she tells them, "I'm going to save the planet." And that is what she knows her calling to be. "The best way to change the world is to lead by example and show people just how wonderful being simple, ethical, and healthy can be!" She doesn't know where she'll be in ten years, let alone two, but she knows that she will always be vegan and will forever be crusading to

raise awareness about respect for all of life, and in so doing will do her small part in "saving the planet."

Duncan Myers

Duncan resides in Grand Haven, Michigan. He holds a Marketing degree from Michigan State University. He is the founder of the Vegetarian Society of West Michigan and remains its director. Duncan is a bartender and also works part-time at a health food store. He enjoys catering vegan parties and volunteering at the local animal shelter.

Ingrid Newkirk

Ingrid founded People for the Ethical Treatment of Animals (PETA) in 1980 out of her basement home. It has grown to over three quarters of a million members and supporters moved to stop the suffering of animals. PETA's motto is "Animals are not ours to eat, wear, experiment on, or use for entertainment." She is the author of half a dozen books in several languages, including *Save the Animals! 251 Simple Things You Can Do*, *Free the Animals! The Inside Story of the Animal Liberation Front in America*, *250 Things You Can Do to Make Your Cat Adore You* and *Kids Can Save the Animals*. Ingrid not only achieved the first criminal conviction of an animal experimenter in the United States, but has traveled all over the world, besieging fur shows in France, helping pass Taiwan's first anti-cruelty law, and saving India's cows.

Alexis Preisser

Alexis is an avid animal and nature lover and has been a vegetarian since she was a small child. She is forty-seven years old and one of the healthiest and most active people around.

Michelle A. Rivera

Michelle is a full-time humane educator and writer living in Jupiter, Florida with her husband, attorney John Rivera, two children, and four companion animals. Her essays on animals have been published in *Animal Writes*, *Animals' Voice*, *Good Dog Magazine*, and *Veterinary Technician* magazine. She has been involved in pet therapy for many years and is a state-certified humane officer, cruelty investigator, and a member of several humane society and rescue alliances. She is also the founder of the Prayer Alliance for Animals. She is the author of *Hospice Hounds: Animals and Healing at the Borders of Death* (Lantern Books, 2001).

Michelle Schreiber

Born and raised in Cleveland, Ohio, Michelle has always reached out to help needy animals. She joined People for the Ethical Treatment of Animals (PETA) in 1996. During her work there, she managed the general operations of the policy department and played a supporting role in many vital projects, including helping PETA to encourage Taiwan to pass its first anti-animal cruelty law. Michelle is currently taking a break from the organization to raise her brand-new, vegan baby girl and to begin creation of a vegan cookbook. She currently resides with her husband and four rescued cats in Suffolk, Virginia.

Richard H. Schwartz, Ph.D.

Richard is Professor Emeritus of Mathematics at the College of Staten Island. He is the author of *Judaism and Vegetarianism*, *Judaism and Global Survival*, and *Mathematics and Global Survival*. He has over 100 articles on the Internet at schwartz.enviroweb.org and at jewishveg.com. He frequently contributes articles and speaks to groups about vegetarian-related issues.

Justin Sivey

Since his early twenties, Justin has been committed to the cruelty-free, vegan lifestyle. He remains indebted to, and draws inspiration from, all of his heroes in this movement, too many to be named. Because of his commitment to a truly cruelty-free world, one of his main interests continues to be informative activism. His other interests include botany, hiking, reading, walking, and philosophy.

Dave Snowdon

Dave is a computer science researcher who lives and works in Grenoble, France and who specializes in human-computer interfaces, computer graphics, virtual reality, and collaborative working. He is also a keen amateur guitar and violin player and writes short fiction. Another of his interests is the use of computers for artistic purposes and he helped stage events in both the NOW 96 and NOW 97 arts festivals in Nottingham, England. More recently, he has been working with Lawrence Ball on Visual Harmony, a program designed to produce graphics and music following the principles of harmonic maths. This work was premiered in a concert in London on November 19, 2000.

Doris Schack

Doris lives in Lincoln, Nebraska with her daughter, two dogs, and ten cats. She has demonstrated at Boys Town to protest their experiments on cats and frequently demonstrates at circuses.

Laurie Crawford Stone

Laurie is an attorney and President of Animal Advocates of Iowa, an Iowa non-profit organization. She is co-founder of AAI. She has worked for several NYSE and NASDAQ companies, most recently as Senior Vice-President and General Counsel. She lives with her husband and seven cats in Cedar Rapids, Iowa.

Veda Stram

Veda was born and has lived in California her entire life. After college, she worked for five years with teenaged delinquent girls in a residential setting. Then she worked temporary administrative jobs to pay the bills while she spent her life at open-air rock concerts and at the beaches and rivers in Santa Barbara throughout the 1970s. Since 1988, she has worked for animal rights, volunteering with Orange County People for Animals, OCPA (www.ocpa.net), since 1996.

Jane Velez-Mitchell

Jane is a TV news journalist and the recipient of two Los Angeles-area Emmys, one New York-area Emmy and four Southern California Golden Mike awards. She has anchored and reported at KCAL-TV Channel 9 in LA for the last decade and previously at WCBS-TV Channel 2 in New York for eight years. She also spent years as a TV journalist in Philadelphia, Minneapolis, and Fort Myers, Florida. Jane founded VegTV.com to combine her passion for vegetarianism with her knowledge of video production and journalism. VegTV.com has just begun producing "video demonstrations" for health-related and cruelty-free products and has begun syndicating its content to other sites on the Internet.

Maru Vigo

Maru emigrated from Peru in 1986 and is currently living in Tucson, Arizona. He holds degrees in Modern Languages, with majors in Spanish, English, and French, and Education. He has been an educator and professional translator for sixteen years. He is active in many other local and international animal organizations. He is a docent at the Humane Society of Southern Arizona where he was honored in 1998 as Teacher of the Year and in 1999 with the Humane Education Award. He is the USA chairperson for Alternativa para la Liberacion Animal (ALA), a Spanish-based animal rights group that covers all animal issues, with an emphasis on bullfighting. He is also a correspondent for the British magazine *The Ark*.

Patrick West

Patrick has been a vegetarian for about four years now and a vegan for two years. His wife, Krista, is also a vegan, as is their three-year-old son

Christopher, who has been a vegan his whole life. Patrick is Director of the Consumer Coalition for Food Labeling, a state-wide, grassroots organization working towards the labeling of genetically engineered foods. He is also the Chairman of the Natural Law Party of Colorado, a nationwide, alternative political party that promotes sustainable living through scientifically proven solutions to health care, crime, education, the environment, foreign policy, economic policy, and more (www.natural-law-colorado.org).

❧ *Voices from the Garden* ❧
A New Crop

We encourage and invite all readers of *Voices from the Garden* to submit their own tales, especially those for whom this book may have been a turning point in their decision to "go vegetarian!"

We look forward to receiving and reading your stories for *Voices from the Garden: A New Crop*. (Please include your name and address.)

Send your stories to:
Daniel and Sharon Towns
c/o Lantern Books
1 Union Square West, Suite 201
New York, NY 10003-3303
USA

❧ *Resources* ❧

American Vegan Society
P.O. Box H
56 Dinshah Lane
Malaga, NJ 08328-0908
T: 856-694-2887

The Animals' Agenda
1301 S. Baylis Street, Suite 325
Baltimore, MD 21224
www.animalsagenda.org

The Animals' Voice
1354 East Ave. #252
Chico, CA 95926
www.animalsvoice.com

Best Friends Animal Sanctuary
5001 Angel Canyon Dr.
Kanab, UT 84741-5001
www.bestfriends.org

Compassion Over Killing
P.O. Box 9773
Washington, DC 20016
www.cok-online.org

EarthSave International
1509 Seabright Avenue, Suite B1
Santa Cruz, CA 95062
www.earthsave.org

FARM
PO Box 30654
Bethesda, MD 20824
www.farmusa.org

Farm Sanctuary
3100 Aikens Rd., P.O. Box 150
Watkins Glen, NY 14891
www.farmsanctuary.org

Friends of Animals
777 Post Road
Darien, CT 06820
www.friendsofanimals.org

The Fund for Animals
200 W. 57th St.
New York, NY 10019
www.fund.org

The Humane Society of the U.S.
2100 L St. N.W.
Washington, DC 20037
www.hsus.org

In Defense of Animals
131 Camino Alto, Ste. E
Mill Valley, CA 94941
www.idausa.org

International Vegetarian Union
P.O. Box 9710
Washington, DC 20016
www.ivu.org

North American Vegetarian Society
P.O. Box 72
Dolgeville, NY 13329
www.navsonline.org

People for the Ethical
Treatment of Animals
501 Front St.
Norfolk, VA 23510
www.peta.org

Performing Animal Welfare Society
P.O. Box 849, Galt, CA 95632
www.pawsweb.org

Physicians Committee
for Responsible Medicine
5100 Wisconsin Ave. NW, Suite 404
Washington, DC 20016
www.pcrm.org

PIGS, a sanctuary
P.O. Box 629
Charles Town, WV 25414
www.pigs.org

Satya: A Magazine of
Vegetarianism, Environmentalism,
and Animal Advocacy
P.O. Box 138, New York 10012
www.satyamag.com

Showing Animals Respect
and Kindness
P.O. Box 28, Geneva, IL 60134
www.sharkonline.org

United Poultry Concerns
P.O. Box 150
Machipongo, VA 23405-0150
www.upc-online.org

Vegan.com
www.vegan.com

Vegan Action
PO Box 4353, Berkeley CA 94704
www.vegan.org

Vegan Outreach
211 Indian Dr
Pittsburgh, PA 15238
www.veganoutreach.org

The Vegan Society
Donald Watson House
7 Battle Road
St. Leonards-on-Sea
East Sussex, TN37 7AA, UK
www.vegansociety.com

Vegetarian Resource Group
and Vegetarian Journal
P.O. Box 1463
Baltimore, MD 21203
www.vrg.org

Vegsource.com
www.vegsource.com

Vegetarian Times
9 Riverbend Drive South
Stamford, CT 06907
www.vegetariantimes.com

Vegnews
P.O. Box 2129
Santa Cruz CA 95063
www.vegnews.com

Vivavegie Society
P.O. Box 294
Prince Street Station
New York, NY 10012
www.vivavegie.org

Vegetarian Society
of the United Kingdom
Parkdale, Dunham Rd.
Altrincham, Cheshire WA14 4QG
England
www.vegsoc.org

❧ *For Further Reading* ❧

Adams, Carol J. *The Inner Art of Vegetarianism: Spiritual Practices for Body and Soul.* New York: Lantern Books, 2000.

——. *The Inner Art of Vegetarianism Workbook: Spiritual Practices for Body and Soul.* New York: Lantern Books, 2001.

——. *Living Among Meat-Eaters.* New York: Three Rivers Press, 2001.

——. *Meditations on The Inner Art of Vegetarianism: Spiritual Practices for Body and Soul.* New York: Lantern Books, 2001.

——. *The Sexual Politics of Meat: A Feminist-Vegetarian Critical Theory.* New York: Continuum, 1999.

Akers, Keith. *A Vegetarian Sourcebook.* Denver, CO: Vegetarian Press, 1993.

Allrich, Karri. *Recipes from a Vegetarian Goddess.* St. Paul, MN: Llewellyn Publications, 2000.

——. *Vegetariana: A Rich Harvest of Wit, Lore, and Recipes.* Rochester, England: Amberwood Press, 1999.

Atlas, Nava. *Vegetarian Soups for All Seasons: A Treasury of Bountiful Low-Fat Soups and Stews.* Boston, MA: Little Brown, 1996.

Atlas, Nava and Lillian Kayte. *Vegetarian Express: Easy, Tasty, and Healthy Menus in 28 Minutes (Or Less).* Boston, MA: Little Brown, 1995.

Avery, Phyllis. *The Garden of Eden: Raw Fruit and Vegetable Recipes.* Vista, CA: Hygeia Publishing Company, 1992.

Batra, Neelam and Shelly Rothschild-Sherwin. *The Indian Vegetarian: Simple Recipes for Today's Kitchen.* New York: Hungry Minds, Inc., 1998.

Beard, Christine. *Become a Vegetarian in Five Easy Steps.* Ithaca, NY: McBooks, 1996.

Beeby, Max and Rosie Beeby. *Cafe Max and Rosie's: Vegetarian Cooking with Health and Spirit.* Berkeley, CA: Ten Speed Press, 2001.

Berkoff, Nancy Ed.D., RD. *Vegan Meals for One or Two: Your Own Personal Recipes.* Baltimore, MD: Vegetarian Resource Group, 2001.

——. *Vegan in Volume: Vegan Quantity Recipes for Every Occasion.* Baltimore, MD: Vegetarian Resource Group, 1999.

Berley, Peter and Melissa Clark. *The Modern Vegetarian Kitchen.* New York: Regan Books, 2000.

Berry, Rynn. *Famous Vegetarians and their Favorite Recipes.* New York: Pythagorean Press, 1993.

——. *Food for the Gods: Vegetarianism and the World's Religions.* New York: Pythagorean Press, 1996.

——. *The New Vegetarians.* New York: Pythagorean Press, 1990.

Bishop, Jack and Anne Stratton. *The Complete Italian Vegetarian Cookbook: 350 Essential Recipes for Inspired Everyday Eating*. Boston, MA: Houghton Mifflin, 1997.

Breier, Davida Gypsy. *Vegan & Vegetarian FAQ*. Baltimore, MD: Vegetarian Resource Group, 2001.

Cadwallader, Sharon. *Easy Vegetarian Cooking*. Bristol Pub Enterprises, 1999.

Costigan, Fran. *Great Good Desserts Naturally!: Secrets of Sensational Sin-Free Sweets*. Summertown, TN: Book Publishing Company, 2000.

Crocker, Betty. *Betty Crocker's Vegetarian Cooking: Easy Meatless Main Dishes Your Family Will Love*. New York: Hungry Minds, 1998.

Davis, Brenda and Vesanto Melina. *Becoming Vegan: The Complete Guide to Adopting a Healthy Plant-Based Diet*. Summertown, TN: Book Publishing Company, 2000.

Devi, Yamuna and David Baird. *Lord Krishna's Cuisine: The Art of Vegetarian Cooking*. New York: Dutton, 1999.

Diamond, Harvey, Marilyn Diamond, and Kay S. Lawrence. *Fit for Life*. New York: Warner Books, 1987.

———. *Fit for Life II: Living Health*. New York: Warner Books, 1993.

Diamond, Marilyn. *The American Vegetarian Cookbook from the Fit for Life Kitchen*. New York: Warner Books, 1990.

———. *A New Way of Eating from the Fit for Life Kitchen*. New York: Warner Books, 1994.

Elliot, Rose. *The Complete Vegetarian Cuisine*. New York: Pantheon Books, 1997.

———. *Rose Elliot's Vegetarian Fast Food: Over 200 Delicious Dishes in Minutes*. New York: Random House, 1995.

Fritschner, Sarah and Linga King. *Vegetarian Express Lane Cookbook: Hassle-Free, Healthful Meals for Really Busy Cooks*. Boston, MA: Houghton Mifflin, 1999.

Gartenstein, Devra: *The Accidental Vegan*. Freedom, CA: Crossing Press, 2000.

Geiskopf-Hadler, Susann and Mindy Toomay. *The Vegan Gourmet: Full Flavor and Variety with over 120 Delicious Recipes* (Expanded Second Edition). Roseville, CA: Prima Publishing, 1999.

Gelles, Carol. *1,000 Vegetarian Recipes*. New York: Hungry Minds, 1996.

Gentle World: *Incredibly Delicious: The Vegan Paradigm Cookbook*. Umatilla, FL: Gentle World, 2001.

Grogan, Bryanna Clark. *The Almost No-Fat Cookbook: Everyday Vegetarian Recipes*. Summertown, TN: Book Publishing Company, 1994.

———. *Nonna's Italian Kitchen: Delicious Homestyle Vegan Cuisine*. Summertown, TN: Book Publishing Company, 1998.

———. *20 Minutes to Dinner: Quick, Low-Fat, Low-Calorie Vegetarian Meals*. Summertown, TN: Book Publishing Company, 1997.

Havala, Suzanne, *The Complete Idiot's Guide to Being Vegetarian*. New York: Alpha Books, 1999.

Haynes, Linda and Jyoti Haynes. *The Vegetarian Lunchbasket: Over 225 Easy, Low-Fat, Nutritious Recipes for the Quality-Conscious Family on the Go.* Novato, CA: New World Library, 1999.

Heidrich, Ruth, Ph.D. *A Race for Life: A Diet and Exercise Program for Superfitness and Reversing the Aging Process.* New York: Lantern Books, 2000.

Hinman, Bobbie. *Burgers 'N Fries 'N Cinnamon Buns: Low-Fat Meatless Versions of Fast Food Favorites.* Summertown, TN: Book Publishing Company, 1993.

Jaffrey, Madhur. *Madhur Jaffrey's World-of-the-East Vegetarian Cookbook.* New York: Knopf, 1987.

———. *Madhur Jaffrey's World Vegetarian.* New York: Clarkson Potter, 1999.

Kalechovsky, Roberta. *Vegetarian Judaism: A Guide for Everyone.* Marblehead, MA: Micah Publications, 1998.

Katzen, Mollie. *The New Enchanted Broccoli Forest.* Berkeley, CA: Ten Speed Press, 2000.

———. *Moosewood Cookbook Classic.* Philadelphia: Running Press, 1996.

———. *The New Moosewood Cookbook.* Berkeley, CA: Ten Speed Press, 2000.

———. *Still Life with Menu Cookbook.* Berkeley, CA: Ten Speed Press, 1994.

Kenton, Susannah and Leslie Kenton. *The New Raw Energy: The Revolutionary Bestseller.* New York: Random House, 1995.

Klaper, Michael, M.D. *Pregnancy, Children and the Vegan Diet.* Umatilla, FL: Gentle World, 1987.

———. *Vegan Nutrition: Pure and Simple.* Umatilla, FL: Gentle World, 1987.

Klein, Donna. *The Mediterranean Vegan Kitchen: Meat-Free, Egg-Free, Dairy-Free Dishes from the Healthiest Place Under the Sun.* New York: HP Books, 2001.

Kochilas, Diane and Vassilis Stenos. *Greek Vegetarian: More than 100 Recipes Inspired by the Traditional Dishes and Flavors of Greece.* Torrance, CA: Griffin Trade, 1999.

Kramer, Sarah and Tanya Barnard. *How It All Vegan!: Irresistible Recipes for an Animal-Free Diet.* Vancouver, Canada: Arsenal Pulp Press, 1999.

Kornfeld, Myra, et al. *The Voluptuous Vegan: More than 200 Sinfully Delicious Recipes for Meatless, Eggless, and Dairy-Free Meals.* New York: Clarkson Potter, 2000.

Lappé, Frances Moore. *Diet for a Small Planet.* New York: Ballantine Books, 1992.

Lemlin, Jeanne. *Main Course: Vegetarian Pleasures.* New York: Harperperennial Library, 1995.

———. *Quick Vegetarian Pleasures: More than 175 Fast, Delicious, and Healthy Meatless Recipes.* New York: Harperperennial Library, 1999.

———. *Simple Vegetarian Pleasures.* New York: Quill, 2000.

——. *Vegetarian Classics: 300 Essential Recipes for Every Course and Every Meal.* New York: Harpercollins, 2001.

Levin, James, M.D. and Natalie Cederquist. *A Celebration of Wellness: A Cookbook for Vibrant Living—Over 300 Heart Healthy, No Dairy, No Cholesterol, Nonfat & Lowfat Inspired Recipes.* New York: Avery Penguin Putnam, 1995.

Lyman, Howard (with Glen Merzer). *Mad Cowboy: Plain Truth From the Cattlerancher Who Won't Eat Meat.* New York: Scribner's, 1998.

Madison, Deborah. *Greens Cookbook: Extraordinary Vegetarian Cuisine from the Celebrated Restaurant.* New York: Bantam Books, 1987.

——. *This Can't Be Tofu: 75 Recipes to Cook Something You Never Thought You Would—And Love Every Bite.* New York: Bantam Doubleday Dell, 2000.

——. *Vegetarian Cooking for Everyone.* New York: Broadway Books, 1997.

Marcus, Erik. *Vegan: A New Ethics of Eating.* Ithaca, NY: McBooks, 1995.

Martin, Jeanne Marie. *Vegan Delights: Gourmet Vegetarian Specialties.* Madeira Park, British Columbia: Harbour Publishing Company, 1997.

McCartney, Linda. *Linda McCartney's Home Cooking.* New York: Arcade Publishing, 1992.

——. *Linda McCartney's World of Vegetarian Cooking: Over 200 Meat-Free Dishes from Around the World.* New York: Bulfinch Press, 2001.

——. *Linda's Kitchen: Simple and Inspiring Recipes for Meatless Meals.* New York: Bulfinch Press, 1997.

McCarty, Meredith. *Fresh from a Vegetarian Kitchen: 450 Delicious Recipes and 75 Menus.* New York: St. Martin's Press, 1995.

McCarty, Meredith and Mague Calanche. *Sweet and Natural: More than 120 Naturally Sweet and Dairy-Free Desserts.* New York: St. Martin's Press, 1999.

McConnell, Shelli. *Better Homes and Gardens Vegetarian Recipes (Cooking for Today).* New York: Better Homes & Gardens Books, 1993.

McDermott, Nancie. *Real Vegetarian Thai.* San Francisco: Chronicle Books, 1997.

McDougall, Mary and John A. McDougall, M.D. *The New McDougall Cookbook.* New York: Plume, 1997.

Melina, Vesanto, Brenda Davis, and Victoria Harrison. *Becoming Vegetarian: The Complete Guide to Adopting a Healthy Vegetarian Diet.* Summertown, TN: Book Publishing Company, 1995.

Messina, Virginia and Mark Messina. *The Vegetarian Way: Total Health for You and Your Family.* Baltimore, MD: Vegetarian Resource Group, 1996.

Migliaccio, Janice Cook. *Follow Your Heart's Vegetarian Soup Cookbook.* Santa Barbara, CA: Woodbridge Press, 1983.

Mitchell, Paulette. *The 15-Minute Gourmet: Vegetarian.* New York: Hungry Minds, 1999.

———. *Vegetarian Sandwiches: Fresh Fillings for Slices, Pockets, Wraps, and Rolls.* San Francisco: Chronicle Books, 2000.

Moosewood Collective. *Sundays at Moosewood Restaurant.* Ithaca, NY: Fireside, 1990.

Murti, Vasu. *They Shall Not Hurt or Destroy: Animal Rights and Vegetarianism in the Western Religious Traditions.* Available from 30 Villanova Lane, Oakland, CA 94611, 1995. Also www.jesusveg.org

Newkirk, Ingrid. *Free the Animals: The Amazing True Story of the Animal Liberation Front.* New York: Lantern Books, 2000.

———. *You Can Save the Animals: 251 Ways to Stop Thoughtless Cruelty.* Roseville, CA: Prima Publishing, 1999.

Padmanabhan, Chandra. *Dakshin: Vegetarian Cuisine from South India.* Boston, MA: Periplus Editions, 1999.

Raichlen, Steven. *Steven Raichlen's High-Flavor, Low-Fat Vegetarian Cooking.* New York: Penguin, 1997.

Raymond, Jennifer. *The Peaceful Palate: Vegetarians' Favorite Cookbook.* Baltimore, MD: Vegetarian Resource Group, 1996.

Rivera, Michelle A. *Hospice Hounds: Animals and Healing at the Borders of Death.* New York: Lantern Books, 2001.

Robertson, Laurel et al. *The New Laurel's Kitchen: A Handbook for Vegetarian Cookery and Nutrition.* Berkeley, CA: Ten Speed Press, 1986.

Robbins, John. *Diet for a New America.* Novato, CA: H. J. Kramer, 1995.

———. *The Food Revolution.* Berkeley, CA: Conari, 2001.

———. *May All Be Fed: A Diet for a New World (Including Recipes by Jia Patton and Friends).* New York: Avon Books, 1993.

Rosen, Steven, ed. *Diet for Transcendence: Vegetarianism and the World Religions.* Badger, CA: Torchlight, 1996.

Rowe, Martin, ed. *The Way of Compassion: Survival Strategies for a World in Crisis.* New York: Stealth Technologies, 1999.

Sacharoff, Shant Nimbark. *Flavors of India: Vegetarian Indian Cuisine.* Summertown, TN: Book Publishing Company, 1996.

Sahni, Julie. *Classic Indian Cooking.* New York: William Morrow, 1980.

———. *Classic Indian Vegetarian and Grain Cooking.* New York: William Morrow, 1985.

Saltzman, Joanne. *Romancing the Bean: Essentials for Creating Vegetarian Bean Dishes.* Novato, CA: H. J. Kramer, 1993.

Saltzman, Joanne and Jay Harlow. *Amazing Grains: Creating Vegetarian Main Dishes with Whole Grains.* Novato, CA: H. J. Kramer, 1990.

Sass, Lorna J. *Lorna Sass' Complete Vegetarian Kitchen: Where Good Flavors and Good Health Meet.* New York: Quill, 1995.

———. *Great Vegetarian Cooking Under Pressure: Two-Hour Taste in Ten Minutes.* New York: William Morrow, 1994.

———. *Lorna Sass' Short-Cut Vegetarian: Great Taste in No Time.* New York: William Morrow, 1997.

———. *The New Vegan Cookbook: Innovative Vegetarian Recipes Free of Dairy, Eggs, and Cholesterol.* San Francisco: Chronicle Books, 2001.

Saturo, Sata. *Chef Sato's All-Natural Desserts: Cakes, Pies, Pastries, and Other Irresistible Sweets.* Becket, MA: One Peaceful World Press, 1998.

Schwartz, Richard. *Judaism and Vegetarianism.* New York: Lantern Books, 2001.

Shaw, Diana and Kathy Warinner. *The Essential Vegetarian Cookbook: Your Guide to the Best Foods on Earth—What to Eat, Where to Get It, How to Prepare It.* New York: Clarkson Potter, 1997.

Shivraj, Manju. *The Spice Box: A Vegetarian Indian Cookbook.* Freedom, CA: Crossing Press, 1990.

Singer, Peter. *Animal Liberation.* New York: Avon, 1991.

Solomon, Jay. *Lean Bean Cuisine: Over 100 Tasty Meatless Recipes from Around the World.* Roseville, CA: Prima Publishing, 1994.

———. *150 Vegan Favorites: Fresh, Easy, and Incredibly Delicious Recipes You Can Enjoy Every Day.* Roseville, CA: Prima Publishing, 1998.

———. *Vegetarian Soup Cuisine: 125 Soups and Stews from Around the World.* Roseville, CA: Prima Publishing, 1996.

Sommerville, Anne. *Fields of Greens: New Vegetarian Recipes from the Celebrated Greens Restaurant.* New York: Bantam Doubleday Dell, 1993.

Spencer, Colin. *The Heretic's Feast: A History of Vegetarianism.* Hanover, NH: University Press of New England, 1995.

Spitler, Sue. *1,000 Low-Fat Vegetarian Recipes.* Chicago: Surrey Books, 2000.

Stepaniak, Joanne, M.S., ed. *The Saucy Vegetarian: Quick & Healthful No-Cook Sauces & Dressings.* Summertown, TN: Book Publishing Company, 2000.

———. *Table for Two: Meat- and Dairy-Free Recipes for Two.* Summertown, TN: Book Publishing Company, 1996.

———. *The Uncheese Cookbook: Creating Amazing Dairy-Free Cheese Substitutes and Classic "Uncheese" Dishes.* Summertown, TN: Book Publishing Company, 1994.

———. *The Vegan Sourcebook.* Lincolnwood, IL: Lowell House, 1998.

——— and Suzanne Havala. *Vegan Vittles: Recipes Inspired by the Critters of Farm Sanctuary.* Summertown, TN: Book Publishing Company, 1996.

Stahler, Charles and Debra Wasserman. *Meatless Meals for Working People: Quick and Easy Vegetarian Recipes.* Baltimore, MD: Vegetarian Resource Group, 1998.

Thomas, Anna. *The New Vegetarian Epicure: Menus for Family and Friends.* New York: Knopf, 1996.

———. *The Vegetarian Epicure.* New York: Random House, 1972.

Vegetarian Times. *Vegetarian Times Beginner's Guide.* New York: Hungry Minds, 1996.

———. *Vegetarian Times Complete Cookbook.* New York: Hungry Minds, 1995.

———. *Vegetarian Times Low-Fat & Fast: 150 Easy Meatless Recipes.* New York: Hungry Minds, 1996.

———. *Vegetarian Times Low-Fat & Fast Asian: 150 Easy Meatless Recipes.* New York: Hungry Minds, 1997.

Vitell, Bettina and Susan Morningstar. *A Taste of Heaven and Earth: A Zen Approach to Cooking and Eating with 150 Satisfying Vegetarian Recipes.* New York: Harperperennial, 1993.

Walters, Kerry S. and Lisa Portmess, eds. *Ethical Vegetarianism: From Pythagoras to Peter Singer.* Albany, NY: SUNY Press, 1999.

———. *Religious Vegetarianism: From Hesiod to the Dalai Lama.* Albany, NY: SUNY Press, 2001.

Wasserman, Debra: *Conveniently Vegan: Turn Packaged Foods into Delicious Vegetarian Dishes.* Baltimore, MD: Vegetarian Resource Group, 1997.

———. *Simply Vegan: Quick Vegetarian Meals.* Baltimore, MD: Vegetarian Resource Group, 1999.

———, ed. *Vegan Handbook: Over 200 Delicious Recipes, Meal Plans, and Vegetarian Resources for All Ages.* Baltimore, MD: Vegetarian Resource Group, 1996.

Wasserman, Debra, and Reed Mangels. *Vegan Handbook: Over 200 Delicious Recipes, Meal Plans and Vegetarian Resources for All Ages.* Baltimore, MD: Vegetarian Resource Group, 1996.

Wolfe, Robert. *Vegetarian Cooking Around the World.* Minneapolis, MN: First Avenue Editions, 1993.

Yntema, Sharon. *Vegetarian Baby: A Sensible Guide for Parents.* Ithaca, NY: McBooks, 1999.

———. *Vegetarian Children: A Supportive Guide for Parents.* Ithaca, NY: McBooks, 1995.

———. *Vegetarian Pregnancy: The Definitive Nutritional Guide to Having a Healthy Baby.* Ithaca, NY: McBooks, 1994.

Yntema, Sharon and Christine H. Beard. *New Vegetarian Baby.* Ithaca, NY: McBooks, 1999.

Young, Richard Alan. *Is God a Vegetarian? Christianity, Vegetarianism, and Animal Rights.* Chicago: Open Court Publishing, 1999.